The Power of Then

The Power of Then

How the Sages of the Past
Can Help Us in Our
Everyday Lives

James Bremner

HAY HOUSE

Australia • Canada • Hong Kong • India
South Africa • United Kingdom • United States

First published and distributed in the United Kingdom by:
Hay House UK Ltd, 292B Kensal Rd, London W10 5BE
Tel: (44) 20 8962 1230; Fax: (44) 20 8962 1239
www.hayhouse.co.uk

Published and distributed in the United States of America by:
Hay House, Inc., PO Box 5100, Carlsbad, CA 92018-5100
Tel: (1) 760 431 7695 or (800) 654 5126; Fax: (1) 760 431 6948 or (800) 650 5115
www.hayhouse.com

Published and distributed in Australia by:
Hay House Australia Ltd, 18/36 Ralph St, Alexandria NSW 2015
Tel: (61) 2 9669 4299; Fax: (61) 2 9669 4144
www.hayhouse.com.au

Published and distributed in the Republic of South Africa by:
Hay House SA (Pty), Ltd, PO Box 990, Witkoppen 2068
Tel/Fax: (27) 11 467 8904
www.hayhouse.co.za

Published and distributed in India by:
Hay House Publishers India, Muskaan Complex, Plot No.3, B-2,
Vasant Kunj, New Delhi – 110 070
Tel: (91) 11 4176 1620; Fax: (91) 11 4176 1630
www.hayhouse.co.in

Distributed in Canada by:
Raincoast, 9050 Shaughnessy St, Vancouver, BC V6P 6E5
Tel: (1) 604 323 7100; Fax: (1) 604 323 2600

Text © James Bremner, 2012

The moral rights of the author have been asserted.

The information given in this book should not be treated as a substitute for professional medical advice; always consult a medical practitioner. Any use of information in this book is at the reader's discretion and risk. Neither the author nor the publisher can be held responsible for any loss, claim or damage arising out of the use, or misuse, or the suggestions made or the failure to take medical advice.

A catalogue record for this book is available from the British Library.

ISBN: 978-1-84850-497-4

Printed and bound in Great Britain by TJ International, Padstow, Cornwall.

To Faye and Eileen,
twa bonnie lasses, with love

CONTENTS

CONTENTS

FOREWORD

My aim in this book has been to distil the teachings of some of the wisest individuals of the past and present them in such a way that they might give some practical help or guidance with problems we all encounter in the modern world. At the same time, I hope the book will not only be enjoyable and useful, but also give insights into the lives of a group of gifted, intuitive and often highly eccentric people of ancient, medieval and early modern times.

I like to think that the people I have included – from the medieval English housewife Margery Kempe to the India-born religious teacher J. Krishnamurti – would all regard this book sympathetically, or at least forgive me for any liberties I may have taken in trying to summarize and explain their lives and works. I have included a range of sages, including mystics, philosophers and psychologists.

Some readers might be put off by the specific religious denominations of some of them, or the absence of any denomination, but I have chosen them more for their insights and their ability as 'spiritual explorers' than for their faith. They all had, I believe, open hearts and open minds, and I hope readers will approach them in the same spirit.

It has always frustrated me that the thoughts of the wise men and women of the past have not been more widely applied to the problems of everyday life – coping with monotonous work, dealing with a mid-life crisis, keeping cheerful when the world seems a terrible place to inhabit, and so on – and this was the spur for writing the book. The people featured in *The Power of Then* lived life to the full and reflected fruitfully on the business of living, with all its attendant problems.

Of course, there are no quick-fix solutions to some of our problems. But sometimes if we change the way we think, or if we see things from another angle, a problem may seem different or more manageable, or it can disappear altogether.

The great seventeenth-century scientist Sir Isaac Newton, referring to his achievements, once wrote: 'If I have seen further it is only by standing on the shoulders of giants.' I like to think that the lives and hard-won wisdom of the sages of the past can also lift us up and enable us to look down on our difficulties with a different, more creative perspective.

A number of people have helped me in the writing of this book by offering encouragement and suggestions, and I would like to thank them all, particularly Siobhan MacKay, Felicity Warner, Ian Wild and Jud Weidner, and especially Eveline O'Donovan.

JAMES BREMNER, 2012

MARGERY KEMPE: THE MID-LIFE CRISIS

'You shall be eaten and gnawed by the people of the world just as any rat gnaws the stockfish. Don't be frightened, daughter for you shall triumph over all your enemies.'

THE VOICE OF JESUS TO MARGERY KEMPE

Having a mid-life crisis is like experiencing the mood swings, grumpiness and escapist fantasies of a teenager all over again. The causes are similar – having endured 14 or more years of being told what to do and when to do it, teenagers invariably crave to break free from the nagging adult voice and its demands. When they find they cannot do so effectively, they react and start a phase of reluctant (or non-) cooperation, often marked by sulking and truculence.

Mid-lifers are similarly provoked. After years of being stuck in the same job – with all its dreary office politics, pressure, thwarted ambitions and the like, not to mention the daily grind of commuting – and worn down by monotonous patterns of domesticity, they can feel the Great Routine squeezing the life out of their spirits like a boa constrictor. The difference between teenagers and mid-lifers though, is that the latter are more empowered to do something about being in a rut.

But for many people, taking action when a mid-life crisis strikes remains just a fantasy and they continue with their routines as they have done for decades. Sometimes they will allow themselves pleasurable daydreams about ditching the nine-to-five office job to teach yoga, or running off with a lover half their age, or selling up and moving to France, or taking a camper van around South America. In the last resort, though, the comfort and security of their spirit-crushing routines sap their will to make a break with the past.

But the call for a new life is a powerful voice that we ignore at our peril. Carl Jung, the great Swiss psychologist, said that the second half of our lives is important for correcting the imbalances of the first half.

The trick is to follow the call to take a new (sometimes radical) direction, while at the same time staying true to our deepest principles and maintaining our integrity. This is not an easy thing to do. But the greatest ally and spur we have is time – or the lack of it. A mid-life crisis, whether it occurs at 35, 40 or 50, carries an implied threat: the glass is definitely looking more half empty than half full, and the grim reaper, if not yet sharpening his sickle, is thinking about visiting the local hardware store to buy a new whetstone.

Perhaps we should think of the mid-life crisis not as something to dread but as a natural event we can almost look forwards to. It is a chance to reassess and take stock of our lives and to strike out on a new path, exhilarated by the thought that it is now or never. There is nothing like the metaphorical 'last petrol before motorway' to quicken the pulse.

An excellent example of someone who experienced a mid-life crisis and radically changed her way of living is a medieval English woman named Margery Kempe. Margery spent the first half of her life giving birth – she had 14 children, although we do not know how many survived – and trying to run a business. But she changed dramatically as she approached her 40th year. Prompted by visionary experiences, she felt a deep urge to go on pilgrimages – at home and abroad – to fulfil her spiritual yearnings. This meant a radical departure from the life she had lived up until then. Although she was highly eccentric and often difficult to be with, Margery is, I think, an inspiration to anyone who has a secret desire to become a free spirit.

The woman from Lynn

Margery Kempe's eventful life, recounted in her memoirs, *The Book of Margery Kempe*, began in about 1373. The daughter of John Brunham, the mayor of the town of Lynn in East Anglia, at the age of 20 she married a respectable local man named John Kempe. During her first pregnancy, Margery fell seriously ill and apparently heard the devil tell her she would be damned; luckily, she also received a vision of Christ, who reassured her he would take care of her throughout her life. (Receiving visions was not uncommon in the medieval world, and those who had them were usually given respect rather than being considered insane. Margery was continually prone to different sorts of visionary experiences, arousing a mixture of awe and suspicion in other people.)

In the years that followed, Margery continued to produce children at regular intervals. She also became involved in the brewing and milling businesses, but without great success. At some point she had a profound mystical experience, hearing a 'melody' that was so sweet it seemed to give her a glimpse of heaven. From that moment on she began to take religion more seriously and started praying, confessing and doing penance. She also begged her husband that they might live together chastely, although John Kempe was not quite ready to surrender his conjugal rights.

Even as Margery made, in her view, spiritual progress, she still had to deal with temptations – including the sin of 'lechery'. A mid-life crisis scenario that is entirely familiar in the modern world came about when a local man, whom Margery evidently found attractive, suddenly told her that he wanted to sleep with her. What was a good upstanding Christian wife to do? Thrown into turmoil, Margery wrestled with her conscience and, probably to her own astonishment, she won: she went to the man (we do not know his name) and told him that she was willing to share his bed.

But as luck would have it, by the time she gave her response, the man had changed his mind. We are not told why. But as

Margery reports it (referring to herself in the third person), he didn't spare her feelings: 'And he said he would not [sleep with her] for all the riches in the world; he would rather be cut up as small as meat for the pot.' Hardly a boost to anyone's self-esteem! The man's rejection brought Margery to her senses and eventually she came to feel ashamed. She attempted to ease her mind and heart with prayer and penance.

As time went on, Margery received further visions and messages from Christ, as well as from the Virgin Mary. She was becoming a bona fide mystic, or visionary, and gaining a reputation as someone touched by God. As her 40th birthday approached, her mid-life crisis grew urgent. It seemed to consist of a deep-seated thirst for freedom from the various well-defined roles medieval society had imposed on her, both as a woman and as a wife. And it expressed itself as a profound desire to undertake pilgrimages to holy shrines. Margery came to realize deep down inside that she had to do this for the sake of her spiritual, and probably mental and emotional, health. By 1413 she was ready to enter the next phase of her life.

On the road

Margery's new direction was a dangerous one – in medieval times, a pilgrimage to a holy shrine was anything but a straightforward journey. It involved great risks, especially if the shrine was overseas. Not many people got to leave their villages, towns and parishes during their time on Earth, so a pilgrimage could be literally the adventure of a lifetime.

Maps were practically non-existent and, without street lighting, journeys had to stop at nightfall. If you happened to be in, say, a wood at dusk, that is where you made your bed (records say that some travellers built small wooden palisades to protect themselves from wolves). There were dangers from outlaws and brigands, too, and many wayfarers fell foul of unscrupulous innkeepers, ferrymen and ship owners.

Needless to say, a female pilgrim was particularly vulnerable on the road, but Margery was not deterred. The spirit of freedom, of questing, surged up in her. This was her time – the period when she wanted to do exactly as her inner voice instructed her.

Margery's book contains scant details of her journeys, but we can imagine her trundling across the Somerset countryside in a wagon as she made her way to Bristol, from there to embark on a ship to Santiago de Compostela in northern Spain. Or walking the last few miles into Rome, the Eternal City, and finding her way to St Peter's Church. I can see her mounting the steps that lead to the vast sanctuary, passing stallholders hawking fish and vegetables, and cobblers offering to mend her shoes. The church itself would have been the largest building Margery had ever encountered (one medieval English pilgrim remarked that it was 'as long as a crossbow will shoot').

But the climax of Margery's pilgrimages was surely the holy city of Jerusalem, to which pilgrims usually travelled by boat from Venice. According to a medieval German friar named Felix Fabri, pilgrims entered Jerusalem via what is now called the Jaffa Gate and were guided to the Church of the Holy Sepulchre, which is believed to be built over the sites of Jesus's death and resurrection.

On seeing this church, many pilgrims were overcome with emotion – Fabri says they beat their chests, or sobbed, or lay down on the ground, as still as corpses, while some female pilgrims screamed 'as if they were giving birth'. Margery was used to expressing her emotions openly and loudly, so it would have been a surprise if she too had not shrieked with joy.

On all her journeys, Margery had to rely on finding sympathetic and trustworthy travelling companions to ensure her safety. It was clear, however, that she was not always the easiest person to be with. She continued to receive visions and possessed what was known (rather euphemistically) as the 'gift of tears'. This basically meant that at the drop of a hat (or, in fact, at the sight of a mother holding her baby, which reminded Margery of the Christ child) she would weep loudly in public places, especially churches.

This 'gift' made her something of a liability and Margery's fellow pilgrims often shunned her. In Venice, for example, she met up with some Englishmen she was hoping to travel with, but they soon tired of her eccentric behaviour – her book records that 'they forsook her and went away from her, leaving her alone. And some of them said that they *would not go with her for a hundred pound*' (my italics).

Margery did not let rejection deter her, though, and she stayed true to her vision. She was courageous both as a traveller and as an outspoken critic of the Church at a time when this was a dangerous activity – she was often interrogated, insulted and attacked by the Church authorities in England for airing publicly her thoughts on religion (women were not allowed to preach openly).

During this period a militant anti-Church group known as the Lollards were making their voices heard and causing disturbances and Margery was sometimes suspected of being a Lollard. Her status as an ordinary lay woman would have given her no special protection from the Church inquisitors: in 1309 a French woman named Marguerite Porete had been burned at the stake in Paris for voicing views the Church considered heretical. Closer to Margery's time, Joan of Arc was burned for heresy in 1431. But whenever she was questioned by the Church and civic authorities, Margery stood her ground and impressed everyone with her integrity.

Last journeys

Margery continued to make long journeys of pilgrimage until the age of 60, by which time she had become decidedly frail.

After the death of one of her sons, she escorted his German wife back to her home city of Danzig in East Prussia and took the opportunity to visit holy shrines at Wilsnack and Aachen. Throughout her later travels she was often spurned by her fellow pilgrims, but sometimes shown extraordinary kindness. In her book, she describes occasions when groups of travellers invited her to join them, on the condition she could keep up with them. Inevitably, given her age, she fell behind and had to turn to other pilgrims.

Margery's book gives a good idea of her state of mind after one such abandonment: 'So they [her companions] went on their way and left her there. Night fell around her, and she felt very wretched, for she was alone. She did not know with whom she could stay that night, nor with whom she could continue her journey the next day.' It is easy to imagine the insecurity, anxiety and low spirits she must have constantly suffered.

It is not known what happened to Margery in the end, but it seems likely that she spent her last days peacefully in her birthplace of Lynn in Norfolk. There, she could have reflected on the symmetry of her two lives: the first dedicated to establishing herself in the world and domesticity, the second to questing.

Margery should be the patron saint of the mid-life crisis. Her inner voice impelled her to take up a life of pilgrimage, and she did not falter. The obstacles must have been enormous, but she took time to make sure her worldly affairs were in good order before embarking on her journeys. We do not know much about how she dealt with her domestic arrangements, yet it seems her conscience was clear, and her only consistent enemies were the Church authorities, who were enraged by the presumption of this strange, spiritually passionate and obstinate woman who dared to criticize them.

So, if mid-life is looming closer in your rear-view mirror, the example of Margery may give serious food for thought. This does not mean rushing off on endless pilgrimages, or forsaking sex with your spouse or partner, but it does mean seriously exploring the truth within yourself and finding out what the years of routine have stifled. What would be your equivalent to Margery's pilgrimages?

The Anglo-American poet T.S. Eliot advised that in our old age we should be explorers, not waiting passively for death. Settling for the easy option, for safe continuity, is not really an option. That is the way of suppressed frustration and possible illness. Surely the point is this: if a 40-year-old woman (which in medieval times was an advanced age) can brave the dangers of solo pilgrimage in pursuit of her dream, we can do the same in pursuit of ours.

If you asked Margery for mid-life advice, she would probably say: 'Follow your inner voice, settle your affairs, negotiate with your loved one(s), be prepared to take risks, and strike forth with courage and faith that your path will lead you to fulfil your potential and destiny.'

HENRY DAVID THOREAU: THE BEAUTY OF SOLITUDE

'I have a great deal of company in my house; especially in the morning, when nobody calls.'

HENRY DAVID THOREAU

The poet John Donne famously wrote that 'No man is an island, entire of itself; every man is a piece of the continent, a part of the main.' We are all interconnected because we are all members of the human race. A person's death, Donne said, will diminish each one of us, because we are all part of the same family.

It is true that we cannot survive, or live easily, without being part of a community. We need farmers to produce food, doctors to treat our illnesses, engineers to build roads and bridges, teachers to educate our children, and so on. We also need friends for pleasure and support. Over the years, most of us build up a personal community – a network of family members, close friends, acquaintances, workmates and neighbours – to help us cope with what the poet John Keats called the 'vale of soul-making', which might also be called (less poetically) *life*.

Although people provide us with life's necessities, comfort and consolation, they cannot, ultimately, make us happy (by which I mean feeling peaceful and contented with our lot). Only *we* can do this, by ourselves. Yet sometimes it may seem as if we can only find happiness through another person, or other people, and human company can be subtly addictive. All of us have a need to be liked or loved, and we can only get validation for this through the reactions of others – a smile, a laugh, a pat on the back, a kiss, a hug, a look in the eyes. Just one person's response to us can be enough.

Conversely, being alone can feel unsettling or even downright scary – as if our sense of personal validation is being threatened. We feel reassured by the ready availability of social networking sites and like to hear the sound of human voices, even if they are only in the background. Whenever we walk into a room in which there is a radio, we are tempted to switch it on automatically, not because we are particularly interested in a specific programme, but because the sound of people talking evokes a sense of human contact.

The radio converts solitude into company. Is there anything wrong with that? Why bask in solitude when you don't have to? Why feel lonely when a radio can suck you into a discussion on how to prune your roses, an analysis of the Olympic 100-metres final or a Bob Dylan concert?

Solitude vs loneliness

But before we go any further, we should consider the difference between *solitude* and *loneliness*, since they are not the same thing. You can work in a busy office but still feel lonely because you have nothing in common with your colleagues. And you can be in a desert by yourself but not feel lonely because you are contented with your life. Solitude is an external circumstance; loneliness is a state of mind. Solitude may lead to loneliness, but loneliness may not be cured by company.

I believe that what we really fear is loneliness, not solitude, but that we often confuse the two. I also think that many people secretly want to find out how they would cope with solitude. The fantasy of being self-reliant, of not depending on others, is a powerful one, and my hunch is that part of it may stem from the great existential fear of death and the fact that all of us have to take that final journey from the Earth by ourselves.

As we board the great express train to our last destination, there may be people at the station waving us off, but on the train itself, we are the only passengers. So, every time we are granted, or seek out, genuine solitude we are perhaps in a small way rehearsing for that final departure. In solitude, we test ourselves – finding out how brave we are.

There are other reasons for wanting solitude, too. Interacting with people can be stimulating, but it can also be draining, especially if there are demands made on our ability to listen, console or think creatively. To get away from everyone for a short while, on a walk or in a quiet room, enables us to regain our composure. Everyone needs a bit of solitude from time to time to pause and reflect – retreat centres and meditation courses are founded on this principle. But what about the effects of sustained solitude – not for a morning, a day or a week, but for much longer?

A cabin in the woods

One person who can shed light on the benefits of sustained solitude is the nineteenth-century American writer Henry David Thoreau. At the age of 28 he built a simple house in the woods beside a small lake near his home village of Concord, Massachusetts, and lived there for two years, later recording his experience in a book called *Walden*.

A studious young man more used to the libraries of Harvard University than the lot of a hermit, Thoreau was seeking solitude to write, and to discover what sort of life he should be living. 'I wished to live deliberately, to front only the essential facts of life, and see if I could not learn what it had to teach,' he wrote.

Otherwise, he feared, the distractions of the world and the bustle of living in a community might eventually make him realize, on his deathbed, that he 'had not lived'. For

Thoreau, solitude was not a dilettante exercise but a serious undertaking to find out the trajectory of his life's course.

Thoreau began work on his new home in the spring of 1845. He chose a spot in the wilds near Walden Pond, a place he knew from growing up in Concord, which lay only a mile away. The house was basically one room, with a bed, a table and chair, and a stove. Thoreau fetched his own water, cooked his own food (once a week he would return to Concord to eat with his family or pick up food) and recorded his thoughts, including notes for *Walden*.

It is clear that, from the start, Thoreau relished sloughing the skin of his relatively sophisticated existence: 'Our life is frittered away by detail,' he declared. 'An honest man has hardly need to count more than his ten fingers, or in extreme cases he may add his ten toes, and lump the rest.' And what were the three cardinal virtues he now advocated for others? 'Simplicity, simplicity, simplicity! I say, let your affairs be as two or three, and not a hundred or a thousand.' This was the first benefit of Thoreau's solitude: paring down his life to its essentials.

Another benefit was his increasing feeling of intimacy with the natural world. He struck up a rapport with the creatures around him, learning to whistle in such a way that a woodchuck would come trundling out of the woods to greet him. Squirrels and birds would appear too, and he fed crows from his hand. He also studied the waters of Walden Pond, making note of the habits of different fish.

Solitude sharpened Thoreau's senses and made him more observant, too. Visitors sometimes came to see him, and if he missed them because he was out walking he could tell what age and gender they were from clues – a dropped flower or nosegay of grasses, or the lingering scent of tobacco smoke from a pipe or cigar.

At night, no one passed his way. He was utterly alone and yet he never 'felt lonesome, or in the least oppressed by a sense of solitude'. Except once, when, in a melancholy mood, he wondered whether human company was essential after all. As these dark thoughts arrived, he began to listen to the rain falling outside and felt 'an infinite and unaccountable friendliness all at once like an atmosphere sustaining me, as made the fancied advantages of human neighborhood insignificant, and I have never thought of them since'.

Nowadays it is relatively rare for us to experience nature with the quality of silence that Thoreau enjoyed. The micro-hum of fridges, air conditioning, heaters and computers can take the edge off the quietness in the most remote dwelling place. Not so for Thoreau. As he emerged from his moment of gloom and doubt, his senses were so alert that 'every little pine needle expanded and swelled with sympathy and befriended me. I was so distinctly made aware of the presence of something kindred to me, even in scenes which we are accustomed to call wild and dreary, and also that the nearest of blood to me and humanest was not a person nor a villager, that I thought no place could ever be strange to me again.'

This is getting close to identifying with nature in a mystical sort of way, which may be beyond all but the most determined and sensitive souls in the modern world. Thoreau's sense of loneliness was replaced by a feeling of belonging to everywhere. It reminds me of the words of the medieval Indian poet Kabir: 'If you do not make your soul welcome, no place on Earth can be your home.'

Back to the source

We might think that a man living alone in a wood was not exceptional in nineteenth-century America – land of the pioneer – but Thoreau's two-year sojourn aroused surprise and much curiosity. His friends challenged him: surely he must feel lonely? His reply was that loneliness lies not in the physical distance between two people, but in the gap between their personalities: 'Why should I feel lonely?… I have found that no exertion of the legs can bring two minds much nearer to one another.'

Thoreau also asked himself: 'What do we want most to dwell near to?' For many of us today, that might be a bank, a school, a doctor, shops, somewhere to go for a walk, and so on. Thoreau came to the conclusion that it is not such amenities. Rather, we want to live as close as possible to the 'perennial source of life'. He did not say exactly what this is, but he did give an example – for a willow tree it is water, towards which 'it sends out its roots'.

Thoreau believed that everyone desires to be close to 'the source of life', but what that is will differ for each person. For Thoreau it was the woods and the pond. For others it might be a place where they can garden or walk in the countryside; or it might be the sea or the mountains, a balmy climate or Renaissance architecture. Or it might not be a physical place but an inner place reached by meditation or prayer.

A life of simplicity

Another insight Thoreau gained was that the casual exchange of pleasantries we have with others during the course of a day can lead to staleness and a mutual loss of respect. 'Society is commonly too cheap,' he wrote. 'We meet at very short intervals, not having had time to acquire any new value for each other. We meet at meals three times a day, and give each other a new taste of that old musty cheese that we are… We live thick and are in each other's way, and stumble over one another, and I think that we thus lose some respect for one another.' Solitude, then, can freshen up our relationships with others – a tactical withdrawal may, for a short while, serve us better than the fray of constant interaction.

Thoreau left his cabin in 1847. He later wrote that his 'experiment' in the woods had taught him to trust his dreams and to live with the freedom of what he called 'a higher order of beings'. The key to this freedom was shedding the complications of everyday living: the more a person simplifies life, the more 'the laws of the universe will appear less complex, and solitude will not be solitude, nor poverty poverty, nor weakness weakness'. In other words, we shall see negative things in a new, positive light.

That is what a spell of prolonged solitude can do for us. It can show us that what we deem essential to our lives may not be after all. With this realization comes a release of energy – previously tied up with fretting over life's details – and a radically new perspective. We might, for instance, see the natural world in a different way and value it more. We might also put greater store on our personal relationships, no longer taking for granted the sound of the human voice.

In the woods at Walden, Thoreau spent longer by himself than most of us would be able to do, or would want to do. Even he needed community to survive (he did not make his own clothes or shoes, for example), and was in constant, though infrequent, contact with other people. My feeling is that although we are social animals, we also need solitude, if only to appreciate this.

It is all about balance. Incessant human interaction at work and at home can leave us drained or buzzing, or both; too much solitude might make us too negatively introverted. As a writer, Thoreau was able to channel the long hours of the day into creativity, but not all of us have that or a similar occupation.

We need to gauge how much social interaction and how much solitude we need, so that the one complements the other. We need to be aware of being addicted to the buzz of society – the feeling of being connected to everyone else through the internet and other communication modes of the digital world. Buzz can be a distraction from the silence in which our deepest personal truths dwell, waiting to emerge during a period of solitude.

Thoreau showed us that we do not need to fear being alone and that, indeed, surprising discoveries and insights can arise from it. Solitude can enable us to find our 'perennial source of life', and there can be no greater discovery.

BROTHER LAWRENCE: GOD AMONG THE POTATO PEEL

'With me, the time of business does not
differ from the time of prayer.'

<small>BROTHER LAWRENCE</small>

In our daily lives we tend to divide our time up into 'pleasure' (going to the cinema), 'duty' (the school run), 'chores' (weeding the garden), 'work' (our occupations) and so on. We try to maximize those things we enjoy doing, and minimize the less pleasant or downright odious tasks. How we experience time is thus conditioned by our state of mind. Time can stretch on and on with boredom – while doing the washing up – or it can shrink to timelessness (while being absorbed by a good book).

But if our thoughts are responsible for the quality of time we experience, is it possible for us to *think* in a way which eliminates the 'dead' time – the type that drags its heels? Is it possible, for example, to assemble electronic circuit boards in a factory all day long without watching the clock and switching into a mode of numbness, but rather feeling peaceful, alive and happy?

One man who managed to achieve peacefulness while engaged in the most laborious and dreary of tasks was Brother Lawrence, a lay monk who lived in a Parisian friary in the 1600s and hardly strayed from its kitchens for 15 years. Lawrence was a useless cook, trusted only to peel potatoes and do other menial tasks, yet he gave off such an inner radiance and tranquility during his years at the potato-face that he attracted visitors from all over France. Like moths drawn to a softly glowing flame, the great and the good made their way to Paris to talk to him and to discover the secret of his peacefulness.

Although Lawrence became steeped in the Christian faith, I think the way he approached his daily life has lessons for us all. But how exactly did he feel at peace with such a humdrum existence? The answer is summed up by the title of the book containing the sum of his wisdom that was published after his death: *The Practice of the Presence of God*. Lawrence practised God's presence in whatever he did and as a result, he did not have to switch modes of operating according to the activity he was engaged in. For example, he did not long to be in the chapel when he was in the kitchen, or vice versa.

This ability to entertain the presence of God was not something Lawrence had been given as a natural gift – he tells us that he had to work at it during his first years at the friary. Nor was he, from what we know, an obvious vehicle for enlightenment.

The winter tree

Lawrence was born in the province of Lorraine in the northeast of France in 1614. His given name was Nicolas Herman, but not much else is known about his family and upbringing. The first inkling of a divine vocation came to him at the age of 18, when he suddenly experienced God through nature. He described this mysterious moment:

'In winter, seeing a tree stripped of its leaves, and considering that within a short time the leaves would be renewed, and after that the flowers and fruit would appear, he [Nicolas] received a high view of the providence and power of God, which has never since been effaced from his soul. This view had perfectly set him loose from the world, and kindled in him such a love for God, that he could not tell whether it had increased in above 40 years that he had lived since.'

Despite receiving this revelation triggered by a deep insight into the inevitable rhythm of the seasons, Nicolas did not at this stage follow a religious life. Instead, he joined the French army and fought in the Thirty Years' War (1618–48), a complex, vicious conflict involving most of the great powers of Europe and fuelled by an inflammable mixture of politics and religious ideals. Atrocities were common – peasants were often herded into cities and crops were burned – and famine and disease took a terrible toll.

Nicolas survived the war, but only just. At one point enemy troops took him prisoner and accused him of being a spy. On the verge of being executed, he managed to persuade his captors of his innocence and was set free. He rejoined his fellow Lorraine soldiers but suffered a wound during the siege of Rambervillers in 1635. Invalided out of the war, Nicolas returned home, letting the fighting continue to rage around him.

What effect the war had on the psyche of a sensitive, spiritually attuned young man can only be imagined. Certainly he was plagued for some years with a sense of his own sin. Did he kill or loot, or watch passively as others did so?

When the war ended, Nicolas tried to find a way of life that suited him, but it was a struggle. He attempted to live as a hermit but failed, and then became a footman to a Monsieur de Fieubet, a French government official. But, by his own admission, Nicolas proved to be a clumsy, oafish servant, dropping things and irritating his employer.

Calm in the kitchen

Then, at the age of 26, Nicolas found his vocation. In the summer of 1640 he entered a Carmelite friary in Paris as a lay brother, taking the religious name of Brother Lawrence of the Resurrection. After two years as a novice, he made his solemn profession of vows. Lawrence was expected to base his life around a regimen of prayer and manual work, and for 15 years he was confined to the friary's kitchen. Temperamentally unsuited to cooking – as he himself stated – he nevertheless found himself preparing food for as many as 100 people a day.

It was a true test of Lawrence's spiritual resolve and patience. We must imagine him picking potatoes out of water, scrubbing them and then cutting them up, or peeling onions, hour after hour. Yet it was during these long, tedious days that he felt God was as close to him as if he were praying in a chapel.

Lawrence found the spiritual life difficult to begin with. He was filled with a great sense of sin, and experiencing God was more an aspiration than a constant reality. So how did he come to feel His presence in his life? Lawrence reported that at the start of his novitiate he devoted the hours appointed for private prayer to just *thinking* about God – to convince himself of God's existence and to impress Him on his heart. For him, faith and devotion were more powerful than reasoning and formal meditation for nurturing a sense of the divine. But the will was important, too. Lawrence resolved to live with a continual sense of God's presence, and '*never to forget him*'.

After he had filled his mind with God during prayer time, Lawrence would take up his post in the kitchen. He brought God with him. It was as if he had taken a giant deep breath and filled his lungs with the divine essence, which sustained him for the remainder of the day. In the kitchen he would think about the jobs that needed to be done and then dedicate the work to God. He prayed for help to concentrate on his tasks, and the grace to continue to be in God's presence. And as he went about his jobs, he kept up an informal conversation with God, treating Him as if He were a kitchen companion.

When he had completed his duties, Lawrence reflected on how he had performed them. If he thought he had done a good job, he gave thanks to God; if not, he asked for his pardon. The crucial thing was this: irrespective of whether or not he felt he had done his work well, he did not praise or criticize himself, but simply continued being in the presence of God. It was as if praise or criticism would have broken the divine spell by introducing the voice of the human self.

Through giving himself to God – opening up to His grace and loving presence – Lawrence reached a remarkable inner peacefulness. His face was noticeably relaxed and calm and this affected the people around him. He never rushed or dallied, but performed the right task at the right moment, always composed and serene. He said that his time in the kitchen was no different from the time of prayer. Even when there was mayhem in the kitchen, he possessed God 'in as great tranquility as if I were upon my knees at the Blessed Supper'.

Lawrence's letters and reported conversations emphasize this simple but powerful idea of being present in God. In Letter One he says he fixed his attention on the holy presence and whenever his mind wandered away – as he acknowledged it inevitably did – he returned it to God: 'For at all times, every hour, every minute, even in the height of my business, I drove away from my mind everything that was capable of interrupting my thought of God.' In doing this, Lawrence felt 'a holy freedom' and a 'familiarity with God'.

In Letter Two he talks of his soul having an ongoing, silent and secret conversation with God, which often caused him to enter a rapturous state. In Letter Six he says that he would try to keep God deep in the centre of his soul for as long as he could – while he did so, he feared nothing, but the slightest turning away from God was intolerable.

Simplicity and prayer

Lawrence continually stresses the need for simplicity when practising the presence of God. In Letter Eight he advises against using a lot of words in prayer. Words, by their very nature, can lead to various mental associations, causing the mind to wander away from God. Instead, he says, we should pray to God 'like a dumb or paralytic beggar at a rich man's gate'. If the mind strays, we must not criticize ourselves, since that will only lead to more turbulence. The will must gently bring the mind back to tranquility.

One way of keeping the mind from straying during prayer time is not to let it go too far away from God at other times. Lawrence repeatedly tries to convey the idea that prayer should be continual – not reserved only for certain places and certain times. He also believed that continual prayer would alleviate physical ailments, although he notes that God does allow us to suffer in order to purify our souls and lead us towards him.

With regard to bodily problems, Lawrence was speaking from firsthand experience. He suffered a great deal of pain in his leg (possibly from a damaged sciatic nerve – the result of a war wound), so much so that after 15 years he was excused from cooking duties. His Carmelite superiors realized that it would be kinder to let him work at something where he could sit down.

So Lawrence became a cobbler, repairing the sandals of his brethren. Again, like his labours in the kitchen, Lawrence's work must have been outwardly monotonous and tedious, but by that time his ability to live in the presence of God was second nature.

Lawrence did occasionally leave the confines of the friary. On one occasion, in 1665, he was sent on a 480-km (298-mile) journey to Auvergne on friary business. The following year he made a 724-km (450-mile) round trip to Burgundy by river. However, his leg was so bad on the latter excursion that he could only get about on the boat 'by rolling over the barrels'. Towards the end of his life, Lawrence suffered increasing pain in his leg, but his communion with God enabled him to bear this trial with good grace. He died on 12 February 1691, at the age of 77.

Lawrence's message to us is clear. Do not place God, or the divine, and 'the rest of life' into separate compartments. God is not confined to the church, temple or shrine only at certain times. Prayer is a constant activity – a conversation with God that takes place no matter what we are doing. And by entering into such a dialogue, we transform the activity we are engaged in.

Peeling potatoes is dull, but peeling potatoes for God, with God, and while talking to God is a holy occupation, and one that has no qualitative difference to praying in a candlelit chapel. Many of us in nine-to-five jobs 'live' for our two or three weeks' annual holiday, thereby creating a tension between 'alive' time and 'dead' time. What would happen if we valued work and holidays equally?

Preparing food, washing, even eating, are times when we often reach for the radio to alleviate the monotony of a routine that requires little thought. But listening to the radio – or to someone on the phone with half an ear – while doing these tasks can easily promote distraction rather than serenity.

Lawrence suggests that if we replace distraction with God, or an inner spiritual guide, treating Him as a friend who is kindly, helpful, loving and full of infinite wisdom, we connect ourselves to a source that soothes the nagging, fretful ego – the ego impatient with the task it has to do. Then, at the end of the work, we emerge as serenely as if we had been meditating in a peaceful room, or sitting outside listening to birdsong.

PLATO: PRISONERS IN THE CAVE

'We can easily forgive a child who is afraid of the dark; the real tragedy of life is when men are afraid of the light.'

PLATO

The question of what is 'real' and what is 'reality' is a crucial one. If what appears to be a red bus to you looks like a large red whale to me, there is a problem. One of us is probably wrong. And it is likely that our particular idea of 'reality' will shape the way we live our lives. For example, if I believe there is no supernatural reality, and therefore no God, my whole outlook, and the way I conduct myself, might differ radically from someone who does believe in its existence.

The words 'real' and 'reality' come from the Latin *res*, meaning 'thing', and they are used to describe situations, events and things as they *are*, and not how we want them to be ('He never faces up to reality.'). 'Reality' also commonly refers to the world outside us – from teapots and trees to other people and everyday situations – which exists separately from our awareness of it ('She is always in a dream and has lost her grip on reality.'). We would also ascribe 'reality' to the inner world of our own mental and emotional states. When a loved one dies, our grief feels all too real; likewise the joy of falling in love, and so on.

So, reality seems straightforward enough. Or does it? One of the issues about 'reality' concerns the way we perceive things. For example, our senses, which we rely on for information about 'reality', can deceive us. I remember once waking myself up from sleep because I thought I could hear a faint but insistent whistling outside, like a distant bird; it turned out to be much closer to home: a semi-blocked nostril. And many times I've executed a smart sidestep to avoid a dog turd on the pavement only to see it move off in the wind because it was an autumnal leaf. Things may not be as 'real' as they seem.

Another issue with reality relates to language. We tend to use words more imprecisely than we might think. What is the 'reality' conveyed by the word 'coffee'? Is it the beans, the powder from the ground beans, the hot, dark brown liquid in a cafetière, or a cup of the latter with milk and sugar added? Or all of those things? Even harder: what is 'real' love or beauty?

'Reality' is something most of us take for granted and don't think about. We tend to assume the world consists of two dimensions: ourselves (with our thoughts and emotions) and things outside us – our house, family, work colleagues, roads, teapots, horses and so on. We might admit that our senses sometimes let us down, but basically we have faith there is an external world with objects that conform to shapes we recognize. For example, every time we see a car, we don't have to do mental gymnastics to fit it into the category of 'car'.

Reality and illusion

It is probably fair to say that we want the 'reality' of our everyday lives to be ordered, stable and somewhat predictable. A universe in which external reality kept changing would be difficult to cope with. I want to be sure that a chair is as solid as it looks before I go to sit on it. So what are we to make of the spiritual teachers who say that the world – our familiar everyday reality – is not as 'real' as we think it is, and is in fact an 'illusion'?

Buddhists, for example, have a term called *maya* that is often translated as 'illusion' and is usually applied to our everyday 'reality' of objects and things. But as I understand it, *maya* does not mean that the low stone wall at the end of my garden is an illusion in the sense that if I sit on it I will be met by thin air and crash to the ground. Rather, it has more to do with the Buddhist idea that the things of the world – even great solid objects such as boulders – are changing all the time, even though we may not perceive this happening. What we think of as solid and permanent reality is in fact *maya*.

In a different sort of way, the great ancient Greek philosopher Plato also thought that the world we live in is a type of illusion – or not as 'real' as another superior reality. To explain what he meant he wrote a short allegory about prisoners chained up in a cave. It became one of the most influential fables in the history of ideas, and when I first came across it, it gave me a new perspective on what reality is and my attitude towards it.

Plato and his world of 'forms'

Born in Athens in 427BC, Plato became a devoted follower of the philosopher Socrates, a man of great integrity and subtle intelligence. Socrates was not afraid to speak out about moral, social and political affairs, and in doing so he fell foul of the Athenian government at a critical time (Athens was trying to recover from a catastrophic military defeat by its enemy, Sparta). He was put on trial on charges that included 'corrupting the minds of the youths' of Athens. Found guilty and sentenced to death, he carried out his own execution by drinking hemlock.

Distraught at his mentor's death, Plato became dis-illusioned with the political scene in Athens and concentrated instead on philosophy, teaching and writing. His most influential book is *The Republic*, in which he explores what makes an ideal political state and other philosophical ideas.

In his writings, Plato constantly reflected on the nature of reality, and he made famous a world view that consisted of two dimensions. In essence, he believed that everything in our ordinary, everyday world – from people and tables to dogs – is merely a copy of a perfect 'form' (or 'idea' or 'archetype') of itself, which exists in another dimension.

So, my chair with its wobbly leg would have a perfect non-material model – the 'form of chair' – in this parallel world of archetypes. My small pink teapot with the chipped handle, my aunt's large blue teapot and my neighbour's stainless steel teapot would all be copies of the perfect form of teapot.

As well as things, Plato's world of forms also consists of archetypes of abstract qualities, such as courage, beauty and love. At the very top of this universe of perfection is the form of Good, which is almost like an impersonal version of God. Everything we encounter in our everyday world, Plato thought, is a copy of one of the forms. We live our lives dealing with mere copies of the real things – and we do not grasp this unless we become enlightened. And how do we get enlightened? By living like philosophers – not stuck in ivory towers on campuses, but simply thinking and reflecting carefully about things.

Plato believed that it is our life's task to move away from the false reality of the everyday world of copies and ascend to the true reality of the perfect archetypes. We cannot encounter the forms by our senses, or by mental effort; we can grasp them only by what he called 'the eye of the soul', or a special understanding – what we might call intuition.

For many people Plato's world of forms seems intuitively satisfying, even though it may be difficult to believe some of the details of the system. For example, you might find it hard to imagine that in the world of forms there really is a perfect bowl of porridge, the copy of which you eat every day. Yet it is a beguiling thought that, although I have various different tables in my house (one round, some rectangular, others short, most with four legs), there is a sense of 'tableness' about them all, and that this 'tableness' might be embodied by an archetypal table – a perfect blueprint in another realm from which the various instances of table have been copied.

Many also find attractive the idea that there is another dimension beyond our 'sensible' (as in perceived by the senses) world – a realm of perfect models – and that it is possible to access this world through contemplation. Although Plato's world of forms is a long way from a heaven or afterlife of the kind that many religions postulate, it nevertheless has an otherworldly allure that appeals to those of us who feel vaguely discontented with the idea that our everyday existence is all there is.

Imprisoned underground

Plato illustrated his idea of the two realities – the world of perfect 'forms' and our everyday world of copies – in *The Republic*, using the image of prisoners in a cave. In the book, the scenario of the cave is described by the character of Socrates.

Imagine, Socrates says, an underground cave with a path leading upward to the light of the outside world. Inside the cave are people who have been living there since they were born. They know no other reality and do not even realize they are prisoners. They are sitting on the ground chained up in such a way that they cannot move their legs and necks. They can only look straight ahead at the wall of the cave.

Behind these prisoners there is a fire. And between the fire and the prisoners' backs there is a road. So, looking from above, you would see, from left to right: the cave wall, the prisoners facing it, a road, a fire.

A procession of people then moves along the road. They are carrying all sorts of objects – pottery vessels, statues of people and animals made of wood – which they hold up so that the light of the fire casts silhouettes of the objects onto the cave wall. These dark flickering shapes are the only things the prisoners can see. If the people carrying the objects speak, then the echo of their words off the cave wall makes it seem as if the words are being uttered by the shadows.

For the prisoners, Socrates says, truth is nothing but the shadows of the objects on the wall. But what would happen if one of the prisoners broke free of his chains? If that occurred, he would stand up and look round at the light of the fire. He would be distressed by the glare and by not being able to see the parade of objects whose shadows he had witnessed on the wall.

If the prisoner was then told that the silhouettes on the wall were an illusion, and that he was now closer to reality – that is, closer to the actual objects casting the silhouettes – he would deny this and insist that his old familiar silhouettes were more real. And if he were forced to look directly at the heart of the fire, he would flinch at the blaze and return to the comfort of the silhouettes.

Towards the upper world

Furthermore, Socrates says, if the freed prisoner were dragged up the path to the mouth of the cave he would be dazzled by the sunlight and unable to see the objects of the upper world, which, he would be told, were even more real than the objects in the cave casting the silhouettes. But, over time, he would get used to the light. First, he would see shadows cast by things, then reflections in water, then the things themselves. He would then look at the light of the moon and the stars, and finally the sun, not as a reflection, but as it actually is.

Eventually, the prisoner would conclude that the sun is the originator of everything visible in the upper world (and, ultimately, the source of the silhouettes he and his imprisoned friends see on the cave wall). He would be delighted at his newfound knowledge and feel sorry for his fellow prisoners.

If the prisoner then returned to the cave and took his seat once more, he would be blinded by the darkness, being now accustomed to daylight. If he and his fellow prisoners played a game of guessing the names of different silhouettes, he would fail and seem stupid to his companions, who would think his eyes had been damaged by his trip to the upper world. This would make them determined to resist anyone who tried to free them from their chains.

The meaning of the allegory

Socrates then explains the story. The cave represents our everyday world and the condition in which we live. In the same way that the prisoners believe the silhouettes are real, so we believe everyday objects are the most real things we can experience (whereas Plato says they are merely copies of 'forms').

The freed prisoner walking along the pathway that leads up to the sunlit entrance of the cave symbolizes the ascent of the individual soul into Plato's dazzling world of forms. And the things in the upper world that can eventually be seen represent the forms of the objects in the cave. The sun in the upper world represents the form of Good, which Plato says is the universal source of human enlightenment.

Those who reach the stage of being able to see the form of Good find it difficult to return to the world of human affairs (the cave) with all its imperfections. If they do go back down, they can easily make fools of themselves by trying to explain concepts to those who have only a limited understanding.

In summary, the allegory says that we gain true knowledge only when we turn away from our everyday 'unreal' world of copies and train our minds to contemplate true reality – the world of forms, culminating with the 'brightest of all realities', the form of Good.

The story also invites us to consider what our own reality consists of. It suggests that we may live our lives mentally chained up and blinkered, unable to shift away from our own tiny knowledge about existence. We watch shadows all day long, believing them to be real things, almost as if we were watching endless soaps on television and believing the characters to be real people.

In fact, one Plato commentator has suggested that a modern equivalent of the prisoners in the cave would be an audience in a cinema. They sit in the darkness, riveted to the screen in front of them as images flick on and off it – images they temporarily believe to be real, until one of them leaves the cinema into the blinding daylight and realizes that another world exists.

Having outlined a dismal scenario of people living in the darkness of their own ignorance, Plato does suggest that it is possible to move away from it to another dimension – to enlightenment of some sort. The problem for most of us is that we are comfortable with the way we live, with our routines, our prejudices, our likes and dislikes.

Breaking the chains

Whether or not we believe in the strict reality of Plato's world of forms, I think Plato's fable challenges all of us to examine ourselves. Is the world we have made for ourselves the best we can do? Is it the most 'real'? Are we living like prisoners without knowing it? Do we refuse invitations to push ourselves beyond our normal comfort zones? Are we intellectually curious, or do we tend to be blinkered when it comes to other people's ideas and enthusiasms?

The image of prisoners chained to the spot, unable to turn their eyes away from what is in front of them, is a haunting one. The antidote to that kind of reality is to force ourselves to move to another sphere. It might be a physical place, somewhere that would take us out of ourselves, or it might be an activity or spiritual exploration – anything that makes us re-evaluate the little corner of reality we have painstakingly created for ourselves.

As the antithesis of one of Plato's hapless cave prisoners there can be few better examples than the Victorian explorer Sir Richard Burton, best known for discovering the source of the River Nile. Burton always sought to push himself into different realities, whether physical or intellectual. He was not only an explorer, but a writer, a poet, a translator (including of *The Kama Sutra*), a soldier, a spy, a diplomat, an orientalist, an ethnologist, a linguist (he spoke Arabic, Icelandic, Swahili and more than 20 other languages), a hypnotist and a fencer.

In his book *Zanzibar*, Burton said that one of the most uplifting moments in life was departing on a distant journey to unknown lands: 'Shaking off with one mighty effort the fetters of Habit, the leaden weight of Routine, the cloak of many Cares and the slavery of Hope, one feels once more happy.' I can feel Plato nodding his head vigorously in agreement.

Plato's allegory is not just a fanciful story. It conveys profound truths that can inspire us to change our lives and to expand them. For example, you might easily get into a domestic rhythm of not going out much, not travelling abroad, not trying out new things or meeting new people. If that were the case, and you did not feel entirely happy about it, you might recall the image of Plato's prisoner freeing himself and experiencing a new reality.

The urge to ascend to the light is, I believe, part of our spiritual DNA. But because it challenges us, and our deeply engrained habits, we do our utmost to ignore it – consciously or subliminally. It is only when, by chance or design, we get a glimpse of the light, from whatever sphere or activity it might come, that we can suddenly see the contours of *our* cave. We can then decide whether to remain seated, content in our chains, or shake them off and explore where the light came from.

MOTHER JULIAN OF NORWICH: ALL SHALL BE WELL

'You shall not be overcome.'

THE WORDS OF GOD TO MOTHER JULIAN OF NORWICH

The world can often seem like a hostile, toxic place for all but the most thick-skinned of souls. Every era has its own particular crises, and in our own time, the threats posed by melting polar ice caps, tsunamis, earthquakes, civil war, international terrorism and so on seem ever present, like a skull-and-crossbones screensaver on our mental computers. It would be interesting to measure just how much emotional energy we expend fending off thoughts of, say, nuclear catastrophe or oil running out.

Some mental health researchers claim that if we have positive thoughts and engage in even small amounts of social interaction, we can bolster our serotonin (the neurotransmitter that affects our moods) and thereby ward off low moods and even severe depression. By the same token, not enough human contact and negative thoughts – which can easily be induced by the ubiquitous gloomy news on the TV or radio – can act like a depressant, depleting our serotonin.

Certainly, there are times when the forces of darkness seem to be getting the upper hand in the world. When this happens we would do well to adapt US psychologist Timothy Leary's famous 1960s mantra, and 'turn off, tune out, drop in' – the first two to avoid crippling waves of negativity, the last to assume some personal responsibility for doing something positive.

A mantra of optimism is a useful thing to have lodged in the mind when times are troubled, and there is a good one in the poem 'Little Gidding' by the modern poet T.S. Eliot. Eliot lived through the Second World War and spent some of his nights on fire watch in London during the Blitz. He experienced firsthand a civilization hanging in the balance, and his poem reflects the dark days of the air raids.

Towards the end of the poem, Eliot uses the words: 'All shall be well, and all manner of thing shall be well.' They strike a note of immediate optimism amid the destruction that was occurring around him; the phrasing is slightly unusual because Eliot was quoting a fourteenth-century English woman named Mother Julian of Norwich.

Julian (she was named after a local saint) was a visionary, or mystic, and the original words spoken to her by Jesus were written down in Middle English and went as follows, '...al shal be wel and al shal be wel and al manner of thyng shal be wele'. In modern English, this reads as, '...all shall be well, and all shall be well, and all manner of thing shall be well'.

(The translator Clifton Wolters has also given the sense as, '…it is all going to be all right; it is all going to be all right; everything is going to be all right').

The repetition of the phrase 'All shall be well, and all shall be well, and all manner of thing shall be well' almost makes the reader feel as if they are eavesdropping on a thought. The words have a memorable rhythm, like a line from a poem or a refrain in a hymn, and the chiming sound of l's throughout ('shall', 'well', 'all') gives the phrase the slightly hypnotic quality of a chant or a mantra. It is a phrase that once remembered is difficult to forget, and it is a good one to summon when life seems unremittingly gloomy, when you find yourself in a difficult situation, or even when you have woken in the night and can't get back to sleep. The words ooze confidence and faith in a positive outcome, no matter what the problem is.

But why was Julian of Norwich told the words in the first place, and can the circumstances of a medieval mystic have any bearing on our own troubled times?

The anchoress's life

Julian of Norwich was an 'anchoress': a religious who disengaged from the world ('anchoress' comes from a Greek word meaning 'withdraw') and lived in a 'cell' attached to the church of St Julian in Norwich, in England's East Anglia. In the medieval period, anchorites (male) and anchoresses were similar to hermits in as much as they cut themselves off from society in order to live holy lives, pared down to the basic requirements and devoted to prayer.

But while hermits lived out in the open in the countryside, anchoresses resided in an 'anchorage', a room or 'cell' – it could sometimes be two or three rooms – physically attached to a church or monastery. There they spent the whole of their lives, never leaving the confines of their self-imposed landscape of walls, and connected to the outside world only by windows.

One window opened up into the church itself so that holy communion could be received from a priest. Another window (or two) faced the street, allowing the women to receive food and water, get rid of their rubbish and listen to people who had come to confess their sins. Some anchoresses had a servant or two to help them live their lives.

Even with servants, and even with two or three rooms, the life of an anchoress is difficult to imagine. An anonymous thirteenth-century guide to living as an anchoress called the *Ancrene Riwle* gives an idea of the conditions under which such women lived. 'Because nobody will see you,' it says, 'do not worry whether your clothes are white or black; just make sure that they are plain, warm and well-made.'

Self-inflicted penance was not recommended: 'Do not wear... haircloth or hedgehog skins, and don't beat yourselves with a leather whip... nor prick yourselves with holly or briars.' Shoes could be 'thick and warm', and on hot summer days, the women were 'free to move around and sit barefoot'. For the head, wimples were not necessary, but a recommended alternative was a plain warm cape and a black veil. 'It is no surprise that women who want to be seen dress up; but, in the eyes of God, they are more lovely if, for His sake, they dress simply,' the guide says. Rings, brooches, gloves and the like were forbidden.

Julian lived most of her life in Norwich, unseen but dispensing wisdom and solace to visitors (one of whom was Margery Kempe) and engaging in contemplation and prayer. Not much is known about who she was. It seems she was born in 1342 and died at the age of 78, but we do not know who her parents were or what sort of family she came from. She describes herself as a 'simple, unlettered creature', but from her writings we can see she had read the Bible and knew the letters of St Paul.

Plague and war

Any notion that Mother Julian lived a serene life, closeted away in Merrie England, and that her words 'All shall be well…' were born from complacency and inapplicable to our troubled times would be incorrect. She lived during arguably the grimmest epoch of European history and nearly died from a mysterious ailment at the age of 30.

The bitter, drawn-out struggle between England and France known as the Hundred Years' War (1337–1453) had begun five years before Julian's birth and would carry on for another 11 years after her death. An even worse catastrophe, however, was the event that began in Europe in October 1347, when a merchant ship from the Crimea arrived at Messina in Sicily. The Messinians soon noticed something odd about the ship: the oarsmen seemed to be sick or dying and all the passengers were dead. Their bodies had large black swellings in their armpits and groins. The bubonic plague, or Black Death, had arrived in Europe.

For the next four years the plague swept across the continent, its deadly bacillus carried by fleas living on rats. Around 20 million people died – a third of the total population. That is roughly the equivalent of 250 million people dying in present-day Europe. As towns were decimated and villages wiped out, it must have seemed to many that the world was coming to an end. Just imagine what the reaction would be today if a mystery disease was wiping out 60 million people a year.

By 1351, when Julian was nine, the plague had more or less run its course. But her home town of Norwich had been badly affected. In the 1330s its population was about 25,000; by the 1370s it had dwindled to fewer than 10,000. There were further problems throughout Britain, and indeed other parts of Europe. With so many labourers dead, the peasants who survived suddenly discovered they were a valuable commodity and demanded better working conditions and higher wages.

The landowners and other authorities were none too impressed by this assertion of workers' rights and came down heavily on the peasants. Tensions erupted into protests. In France a rebellion called the Jacquerie broke out in 1358, and in England the Peasants' Revolt erupted in 1381, when Norwich itself was pillaged by a band of rebels. The peasants were defeated in both cases, but a sense of social unrest and turbulence remained.

It is inconceivable that Julian would not have had friends and family affected by plague and war, and it is possible that some dark event in her life prompted her to embrace the life of an anchoress. She would have entered her anchorage fully aware of the tragedy and fragility of human existence.

Close to death

Julian's life of solitude began in May 1373 when, at the age of 30, she had a momentous near-death experience, accompanied by a series of visions. She later wrote that she was seriously ill for three days and, having received the last rites, thought she would not survive the fourth night. She remembered the great sorrow she felt, knowing she was going to die. Her body felt paralysed from the waist downward. The curate was sent for.

When he arrived, she was unable to speak. He placed a crucifix in front of her face.

Julian's own words capture the drama of what happened next: 'After this my sight began to fail, and it was all dark about me in the chamber, as if it had been night, except in the image of the cross on which I saw a common light... After this the upper part of my body began to die... I scarcely had any feeling, with shortness of breath. And then I knew for sure I had passed away. And in this moment suddenly all my pain was taken from me, and I was as whole (and specially in the lower part of my body) as ever I was before. I marvelled at this sudden change; for I thought it was a miracle of God, and not of nature.'

Julian was restored to life. She then received the series of 16 revelations (or 'showings', as she called them) that shaped the rest of her life. The first 15 occurred on the day after her recovery, and the last one happened on the following night.

The revelations took the form of vivid images of Jesus and of spiritual truths. Julian seemed to enter an otherworldly realm where she contemplated the great mysteries of existence, including the nature of sin and love. Shortly after the experience, Julian wrote down the essential substance of the revelations, but she continued to ponder them over a period of 20 or more years and ended up writing a longer account, which includes her reflections on their meaning.

The 'showings'

It is noticeable how visual some of her revelations were. Many medieval mystics experienced intense states of emotion without seeing powerful images, but not Julian. Among other things, she saw in graphic detail the head of Jesus wearing the crown of thorns: '…great drops of blood fell down from under the garland like pellets, seeming as it had come out of the veins; and in the coming out they were brown-red, for the blood was full thick; and in the spreading-abroad they were bright-red…' The blood trickled continuously 'like drops of water that fall off the eaves after a great shower of rain' and the drops were as round as 'the scales of herrings'.

In other revelations the visual element leads directly to a spiritual truth. For example, she was shown by God 'a little thing, the size of a hazelnut, in the palm of my hand; and it was as round as a ball'. When she asked what it was, she was told: 'It is all that is made.' When she wondered whether this small ball might disintegrate she was told: 'It endures now, and shall last forever because God loves it.'

From this she concluded that everything owes its existence to the love of God. In other words, even the smallest piece of creation, even a non-human object, has been invested with life derived from the divine source of love.

The theme of divine love making the universe go round is a constant pulse throughout the body of Julian's work. It is one of the many positive notes that makes reading her words a cheering exercise on a dark day. When the serotonin barometer is dropping, it is comforting to know that back in the apocalyptic fourteenth century a solitary soul was keeping her own and other people's spirits up with a benevolent optimism.

Although destruction was all around her, Julian declared that we 'are clothed in the goodness of God', in the same way that 'the body is clothed in cloth, the flesh in skin, the bones in flesh, the heart in the body'.

Mother Jesus

Another element of Julian's writing that is striking and consoling is her description of God and Jesus as a loving and tender *mother*. Julian wasn't the first person to write about the feminine side of God and Jesus, but she was one of the most influential. For anyone used to God being described as a father, it comes as a surprise to find 'Him' being called 'Her' – a mother: 'This fair lovely word *Mother*, it is so sweet... it may not truly be said of anyone but Him.'

Julian's language is full of maternal warmth: 'The mother may give her child suck of her milk, but our precious Mother, Jesus, he may feed us with himself, and does it, full courteously and full tenderly, with the blessed sacrament that is precious food of my life.' In a similar vein, she says,

'...the mother may lay the child tenderly to her breast, but our tender Mother, Jesus, he may homely lead us into his blessed breast'.

While England and other parts of Europe suffered plague, war and social unrest, Julian kept focused on her sense that despite everything, God would be close to his creatures – God who was filled with tender love, like a mother. Even for those of us today who are unsure whether we believe in God or not, the idea of a divine presence being with us wherever we are, and in whatever state we are in, is reassuring.

For Julian, this divine presence was not just a theoretical notion but a lived experience: in one of her visions she felt herself float down to the bottom of the sea, where she saw 'green hills and valleys, as if covered with moss, seaweed and sand'. She then came to the realization that 'if a man or woman were under the ocean and saw God (God being continually present), he or she should be safe in body and soul, and come to no harm'.

No matter where we are, on land or beneath the sea, God is with us. Julian's memorable ocean scenario echoes Psalm 139 in the Bible – a great poetic cry to the inseparable relationship between God and humankind: 'If I go up to the heavens, you are there; if I make my bed in the depths, you are there. If I rise on the wings of the dawn, if I settle on the far side of the sea, even there your hand will guide me, your right hand will hold me fast.'

Love is the source

For a full 15 years after her revelations, Julian wondered about their meaning and what had inspired them. Then one day she suddenly received an answer through a spiritual intuition. An inner voice said to her: 'Do you want to know your Lord's meaning in this thing? Learn it well: Love was His meaning. Who showed it to you? Love. What did He show you? Love. Why did He show it to you? For Love.' It is as if the answer to every question Julian might have asked would be 'love' – as if love is the be-all and end-all of life and is almost the same thing as God.

With this conviction that love is always surrounding us, even though we might be in a dark place, it is not surprising that Julian could utter the words 'All shall be well…' Her positive vision must have made her anchorage a glowing cell of light in those dark times in Norwich and beyond. Visitors would have left her outer window with her words whispering in their memories, full of renewed hope and courage. Julian's was not a bland optimism, but a profound reflection on knowledge revealed to her.

We, too, in our dark times, whether at an international level (like T.S. Eliot during the Second World War) or in our personal lives, can take great comfort from Julian's idea that no matter how bad things get, there is a divine source of love – tender and motherly – that we always have access to, even when we feel at our most emotionally isolated.

Julian felt emotional isolation, which is why her writings are not a dry theological treatise but a sympathetic record of her thoughts and feelings. She records how, soon after her revelations, she went through alternating moods of serenity and sadness. She felt 'heaviness, and weariness of my life, and irksomeness of myself, that scarcely I could have patience to live. There was no comfort nor none ease to me but faith, hope, and charity; and these I had in truth, but little in feeling'.

This 'heaviness' and 'weariness' – what we might call depression – must have recurred. Yet in her darkest moments she would have remembered another phrase God said to her: 'You shall not be overcome.' As she describes it: 'And this word: You shall not be overcome, was said clearly and powerfully, as a reassurance and comfort against all tribulations that may come. He did not say: You shall not be buffeted, you shall not be put under strain, you shall not be afflicted; but He did say: You shall not be overcome.'

None of us can hope to escape what life throws at us, but we can fortify ourselves by absorbing the quiet confidence of Mother Julian and her brief but memorable words.

CARL JUNG: EMBRACING THE SHADOW

'To become conscious of it [the shadow] involves recognizing the dark aspects of the personality as present and real. This act is the essential condition for any kind of self-knowledge.'

CARL JUNG

It's a familiar scenario: the homophobic man who does not acknowledge his own sexual ambivalence; the unaware racist who finds racism in the behaviour of everyone but himself or herself. Those whom we find irritating, exasperating or even hateful often embody a part of ourselves that we are barely aware of and which we project onto or find in other people. The Swiss psychologist Carl Jung believed this unacknowledged or neglected part of us is buried deep within our unconscious mind. He viewed it as a sort of dark, hidden personality and called it the 'shadow'.

Jung said that the shadow appears in our dreams as a menacing figure. Our task is to recognize and come to terms with it in order to stop projecting it onto other people. By becoming aware of the shadow – by making it conscious – we rob it of its power and are better able to correct any emotional imbalances we may have. (One of Jung's favourite examples of what can happen if the shadow gains too much power is Robert Louis Stevenson's story of the good Dr Jekyll turning into Mr Hyde, the evil side of his personality.)

But getting to know the shadow, and coming to terms with it, is extraordinarily difficult. As Jung said: 'In reality, the acceptance of the shadow-side of human nature verges on the impossible. Consider for a moment what it means to grant the right of existence to what is unreasonable, senseless, and evil!'

Because we spend most of our lives conveniently ignoring and suppressing the less attractive parts of our personalities, there is a strong motivation to keep the lid on what we do not like about ourselves. Most of the time we are not even aware there is a problem: if we dislike someone, we tend to think it is *their* fault – they are selfish, thoughtless, careless, brutish, and so on. We may be partially justified in our dislike of someone, but the chances are that the person is reflecting some part of our selves that we have repressed.

But how does the shadow take shape within us in the first place? After all, most of us try to live decent, self-aware lives and refrain from lying, cheating, deceiving, stealing, and so on if only because we know that society would collapse if it were based on such activities. Why should we develop a dark, negative side that lurks in the murky recesses of our psyches?

By and large, we conform to the rules of the society we live in. We recognize that there are not only legal rules (paying taxes, wearing a seat belt), but unspoken ones too, governed by an inner voice. The latter prompt us to be thoughtful (remembering a birthday) and dutiful (collecting money for charity), or to practise good manners (giving up our seat on a bus to a disabled person). So we live our lives according to outer (legal) rules and inner rules.

Parents, teachers, friends and other members of society encourage us, openly or by implication, to be law-abiding, kind, generous, sensitive and polite souls intent on making the world a better place. We would be affronted if we were informed we were not those things. Manipulative, cruel, mean, crass and rude are adjectives we would not want featured on our existential curriculum vitae.

But the problem with being 'decent' or 'good', or *aiming* to be decent or good, is that it takes effort and energy. Ranged against our forces of decency are the armies of Lord Negative: inertia, sloth, selfishness, spite, envy – the list goes on.

This mental and emotional struggle in the battlefields of the mind and heart causes a split. On one side, the voice of conscience urges me to rise from the sofa and make my partner, exhausted after a day's work, a cup of tea; on the other side, the voice of selfishness says: 'Keep your head down. Read the newspaper. Relax.'

It's a struggle as old, at least, as the Bible. St Paul once wrote a letter to the Christian community in Rome in which he explained how difficult it was to lead an upright life. He said: 'It's a mystery to me why I behave the way I do. I know what is right, but I don't do it. Instead I do the things I hate.'

Our motivation to be good and decent is also based on our need to secure or maintain public approval. We respect or fear what our neighbours think of us more than we care to admit.

So there are two lots of pressure (the voice of conscience and the desire for public approval) urging us to be good. At the same time, negative impulses, such as inertia and selfishness, are jostling to be heard and expressed. So what do we do? We squash down and repress those unwelcome, ugly impulses, hoping they will go away or languish impotently in the darkness of our minds. They may indeed languish, but it seems to be a psychic law that they do not go away.

Jung and the unconscious mind

Jung was fascinated by the task of dealing with our dark side. As already mentioned, he believed that if our negative traits and impulses are not acknowledged, they will fester and strengthen in the recesses of our psyches in the form of the shadow. Jung saw this process happening in the context of what he called the 'collective unconscious' – a sort of universal mind. The collective unconscious has far-reaching implications (and still stirs debate and controversy among psychologists): how did Jung arrive at the concept?

Born in 1875, Carl Jung was, along with the Austrian neurologist Sigmund Freud and others, one of the pioneers of what is called depth psychology (a branch of psychology that gives great importance to the unconscious mind). As a child and a young adult Jung was already fascinated by the psychology of others. For example, at an early age he observed how his father, a Swiss Lutheran pastor, struggled to come to terms with his waning faith.

He also noticed that his mother seemed to have two distinct personalities. The first one was conventional and dealt with day-to-day living, while the second would suddenly pop out and utter wise and authoritative statements that were out of character with the first.

Jung studied medicine at the university of Basel in Switzerland and then became an assistant in a mental hospital near Zurich. It was during this period that he came to be influenced by the writings of Freud, his older contemporary (with whom he later fell out over disagreements about theories). Freud had developed the idea that everyone has an 'unconscious' mind, which acts like a sort of receptacle for unwanted, painful memories.

Jung took this idea of the unconscious a step further and developed his own model of it. He believed that the unconscious mind has two parts – personal and collective. Every person has a 'personal unconscious' that is peculiar to him or herself, and which can be accessed through dreams and daydreams. But Jung's biggest difference with Freud was his belief in a collective unconscious.

While treating schizophrenics at the hospital, Jung noticed that their fantasies reminded him of characters and stories found in myths. He began to study the myths of different cultures and concluded there were patterns in these stories that appeared again and again (such as a god turning himself into a human being or an animal; or a trickster figure sabotaging some human enterprise). If the dreams of schizophrenics showed similarities with these mythic stories, perhaps, he wondered, the dreams of 'healthy' people did too?

Dreams were important to Jung. He came to the conclusion that many dreams derive from the personal unconscious and reflect a person's particular issues (such as always being late for an appointment). But he also pointed out that people sometimes have 'big dreams' with a strong mythic content (e.g. dragons, earthquakes, epic journeys).

He believed that these dreams arise from the collective unconscious – a storehouse of symbolic images embodying typical life situations or instinctive patterns (reaching adolescence, for example). He called these instinctive patterns 'archetypal' and the images that arise in them 'archetypes'.

One archetypal pattern is that of the hero and his quest to slay a dragon or other monster to rescue a maiden or save a community. This story is found in myths throughout the world and Jung would say that it symbolizes a universal pattern of human behaviour (possibly something like the need for a young man [the hero] to liberate himself from an overpowering mother figure [the dragon] and establish himself as a fully-fledged adult).

Jung's two-part unconscious – personal and collective – could be compared to a scene in which a number of ships are sailing on the sea. Each ship is different and represents a person's individual mind or psyche. The part of the ship *above* the water is like the conscious mind, with the ship's captain as the ego – able to see, control and guide the ship. The part of the vessel *below* the water is dark and unseen, like the personal unconscious, with barnacles or scratches on it from an accident, or wear and tear, like forgotten memories of wounds or traumas. Both parts of the ships, above and below, form its whole.

But down below all the ships stretches a vast realm of ocean, populated at great depths by fish and other creatures with weird shapes that seem positively prehistoric. This immeasurable expanse of water and its marine life do not belong to any one ship but to all of them. If a diving chamber was let down from each ship, those inside it would see similar sorts of ocean landscape, flora and creatures.

This ocean, then, is like the collective unconscious – the property of no one ship, but underpinning all of them. The living forms within the sea's great depths represent the archetypal figures that feature in the collective unconscious, and which appear in people's dreams and the myths of different cultures.

Enter the shadow

Jung developed the idea of the collective unconscious for most of his life, much of it based on his own personal experience of it. During the years of the First World War he had a kind of self-induced mental breakdown, during which he explored his own psyche in a series of daydreams or fantasies that at times threatened to overwhelm him. But he emerged from the experience and began to write down what he had encountered.

Jung eventually gave names to the archetypal images he found recurring in dreams and myths. There is, for example, the *persona* – the 'mask' that people adopt when they take on specific roles (a doctor might have a persona when at work, and then revert to 'normal' when off duty).

Then there is the *anima* – the image (which takes the form of a female) that represents the feminine side of a man's nature – and the *animus*, the masculine side of a woman. In other words, if a woman dreams about a distinctive male figure, such as a pirate or a footballer, Jung would say she is dreaming not about buccaneering or sport but about getting in touch with the masculine part of her nature.

One of the most significant archetypes is the shadow, which, as mentioned before, represents the part of ourselves we have unknowingly suppressed (because we are ashamed of it), or have disowned or neglected. The shadow is often personified in dreams by a shady, disreputable figure of the same gender as the dreamer. It might be a tramp, an alcoholic, a pickpocket or a confidence trickster. Or it might be a more threatening figure, such as a mugger or an assassin.

Let's look at a hypothetical example. There is a clergyman who believes he is modest and humble but keeps dreaming about a male figure who is proud and ambitious. A Jungian analyst might suggest that the dream figure is the man's shadow and that the dream is telling him he is not acknowledging the fact that he is suppressing his own all-too-real pride and ambition.

Or let's say a headmistress of a college enjoys her reputation for being upright, morally strict and cerebral. She might then encounter in her dreams a female hippy or 'Earth Mother' type whom she finds repellent but who is effectively telling her that she needs to loosen up and get in touch with the more earthy side of her personality.

Jung believed that the more we ignore our shadows, the stronger they grow. 'A small evil becomes a big one through being disregarded and repressed,' he said. The shadows warn us of this by becoming more menacing in our dreams. If we continue to ignore them we may allow them to take us over temporarily (as in the story of Jekyll and Hyde). Less dramatically, this might happen, say, with a fervent 'holier than thou' churchgoer who, out of the blue, has a wild extramarital fling.

Projecting the shadow

Jung also thought that we have an innate capacity to project our shadows onto others (i.e. to see in other people our own suppressed faults). 'Projections change the world into the replica of one's own unknown face,' he said. We know this is happening when we find ourselves unusually irritated, angry or upset over certain people in a way that baffles our friends. We are angry because we see in those individuals the very qualities that we have unwittingly suppressed in ourselves.

So, the quiet, bookish scholar finds outgoing party animals intolerable; the person unaware of his own miserly instincts always notices when someone else is holding back from buying a round of drinks; and the office worker who believes herself to be modest and unassuming is extraordinarily riled by the slightly pushy behaviour of an overtly ambitious colleague.

We all have shadows, and we all project them to a greater or lesser degree onto others. So what can we do about it? The first priority is to recognize what our shadow is like. To achieve this we must do two things: remember those dream figures of the same gender whom we find repellent or menacing; and become aware of individuals who annoy us intensely for no great reason. Jung consistently wrote down his dreams and encouraged his patients to do the same, or to paint pictures of them. Recording our dreams makes us better able to acknowledge and understand them.

Once we have identified our shadow, and the neglected qualities it represents, we can come to terms with it. We have to acknowledge and embrace it. This is the hard part. The shadow is a 'reject' in the unconscious for good reason: we dislike or are ashamed of it. But Jung believed we can only progress on the journey to mental and emotional maturity (he called it the 'path of individuation') by having the moral courage to see and acknowledge our shadow selves.

We have to see through our pretence that we are unfailingly kind, fearless, generous, self-sacrificing, etc., and realize that we have a lot of negative traits too. By acknowledging the shadow we can then withdraw the shadow projections we have cast on other people. If we do that, the menacing dream figures, now that they have been acknowledged, will become less threatening. We will also find that certain individuals whom we irrationally disliked now seem much nicer than we thought.

The work with the shadow is ongoing. We may embrace our shadow at a certain age and then have to acknowledge another (different) one when we are older. It is a lifetime's vigil that requires moral courage, but in recognizing that we may be selfish, mean, arrogant or ambitious we will find the wherewithal to heal our relationships with others – from office colleagues to family members – and to become more mature, emotionally and socially.

JEAN-PIERRE DE CAUSSADE: THE PRESENT MOMENT

'The divine will is a deep abyss of which the
present moment is the entrance.'

JEAN-PIERRE DE CAUSSADE

For thousands of years, poets have lamented our brief span of life, with many of them urging us to concentrate on the present rather than worrying about the future or regretting the past. The ancient Greek poet Homer wrote in the *Iliad*: 'People's lives are like the generations of leaves. The winds scatter the old leaves across the Earth, the trees burst alive with new buds and spring returns. That's how it is with human beings: as one generation comes to life, another dies away.'

This inescapable rhythm of nature is both a comfort (life goes on) and a cause for sadness (we die). By facing up to this pattern of mortality, however, we are better able to enjoy the present. The knowledge that we are going to die, and that our lives are like the leaves the wind scatters as we are eventually replaced by our children and grandchildren, is an incentive to focus on our fleeting time on Earth.

The idea of relishing the present was famously captured in the Latin phrase *carpe diem*, 'seize the day', coined by the

Roman poet Horace in one of his odes. In the poem, Horace addresses a younger woman named Leuconoë and tells her not to worry about the future. She should enjoy the good things in life while she can:

'We can't know what the gods have in store for us, so don't ask, and don't consult the fortune-tellers either, Leuconoë. It's better to put up with what befalls us, whether Jupiter allows us to enjoy a few more winters, or whether this will be our last, as it shreds the sea against the rocks. Be smart: strain your wine, and trim your hopes to match a life that's short. Even while we're talking green-eyed time has slipped away. Seize the day, and trust the future as little as you can.'

The idea of seizing the day – grasping whatever it puts before us, good or ill – remains a powerful motif with poets and other writers and artists. It is also a mainstay of spiritual teachers. Jesus, for example, said that we should not worry about tomorrow 'because tomorrow will worry about itself: each day has enough troubles of its own'.

But it is difficult to seize the day and avoid thinking about the past and the future. We seem to be born with a consciousness that is naturally tuned into the three time categories of past, present and future. They seem to make intuitive sense. It is difficult to pin down the present because it's always slipping away into the past (even as I type these words!).

But the past itself seems fairly clear. It is linked with memory: I can remember the birthday party I had two years ago. I can remember dropping the car off at the garage yesterday evening. Languages have a variety of past tenses, reflecting different types of past action. In English, for example, you can say: I chopped wood; I used to chop wood; I was chopping wood; I have chopped wood.

Similarly, the future as a concept seems intuitively right. It is linked not so much to memory as to speculation, daydream and fantasy. I can picture the committee meeting I am going to next week. I can make arrangements to book a train seat for next Tuesday. I'm looking forwards to the cup of tea I'm about to make, and so on. Of course, whereas the past is unchangeable, the future may never happen. Life can intervene at any moment and thwart our plans. Nevertheless, the idea of the future seems crucial to our lives: how can we plan ahead if we cannot conceive of the future?

Yet, although the three categories of time seem natural and indispensable, there are other aspects of time that appear to be more artificial. The idea of days and nights and months is clearly linked to the rhythm of the sun and the moon (the word 'month' is related to the word 'moon'), but what about the divisions of hours, minutes and seconds on our clocks and watches? The widespread use of clocks is relatively recent (time was largely measured by sundials on a local basis until the late eighteenth and early nineteenth centuries): it took the advent of the railways and the need for timetables to standardize time.

Spiritual teachers advise us to move beyond *all* divisions of time – to stop counting out our lives in units, and to live in the present. To do otherwise, they suggest, is to waste energy either regretting or relishing the past, or looking forwards to or dreading the future. For example, I insult a person at a party and, even though I apologize at the time, I continue to churn the incident over in my mind. Why can't I let the past go? Or, I'm going to the dentist next week and I'm worried I might have to have a tooth taken out. My wife tells me not to fret over something that might not occur, but that doesn't help at all.

And so it goes on: we are pincered by memories of the past on the one hand, and by imagined events of the future on the other.

I know that it would be good to live in the present – in the moment. To be so absorbed in something that you are unaware of time is a blessing. I have only encountered this once or twice, mostly when playing sport, when I had to react so quickly to something that I forgot both myself and time. But to live in the present as a habit is one of the hardest things, if not *the* hardest thing, we can do in life. To do so permanently would be, I suppose, to have reached spiritual enlightenment.

De Caussade's 'sacrament'

So, how do we live in the present? How do we come to terms with the past and the future and create a mind that exists only in the present? This question was explored in the eighteenth century by a French Jesuit priest named Jean-Pierre de Caussade. It might seem strange that someone living three centuries ago should have addressed a topic that is so fashionable today, but De Caussade wrote eloquently about it. He coined the phrase 'the sacrament of the present moment', which captures beautifully the preciousness and holy quality of living in the present.

We only have a bare outline of De Caussade's life. He was born in France in 1675 and joined the Jesuits in Toulouse at the age of 18. In 1708, at the age of 33, he took his final Jesuit vows, and after that he seems to have led a conventional Jesuit life – teaching, preaching and acting as a confessor. At the age of 54, he became spiritual director at a convent in Nancy, in Lorraine, northeast France. He later moved to positions at Perpignan and Albi, before returning to Toulouse, where he died in 1751.

While at the convent, De Caussade gave spiritual guidance to the nuns through personal talks and letters. Some of his conversations were jotted down, and nine years after his death they were published, along with some of his letters, in a book called *Abandonment to Divine Providence*, which was to establish him as a profound spiritual thinker.

Much of De Caussade's writing focuses on the importance of living in the present. As someone committed to a religious vocation, he was steeped in the rules and regulations of Roman Catholicism as practised in eighteenth-century France. He believed that although these rules were necessary in *his* day, they had not been needed by the early Christians – at least not to the same degree. The Church fathers, as they were known, were so absorbed in their duties that they focused on what was before them, 'like the hand of a clock that at each moment covers the space it's travelling along'.

As a Christian, De Caussade believed that God had ordered the world in the best way possible and that whatever happens, good or bad, is providential, working for our benefit. Our sole duty, he says, is to focus on the present moment. We must discard our personal inclinations and feelings and focus on 'the duty of the present moment'.

We must forget the moment before, and disregard the moment to come. By doing this we will realize what is right for us at that very moment – in other words, what, in De Caussade's terms, God has planned for us. The present moment, he says, is the portal to the 'deep abyss' of God's will: if we throw ourselves into that abyss we will find it infinitely vaster than our desires.

Central to taking this plunge, De Caussade believed, is trusting our instincts, or intuition, and having faith that they are prompted by God. Our natural tendency is to plan ahead, to want to be in control. It is difficult to cast ourselves into the blank space of the present moment. It requires a sort of thoughtless spontaneity that for most of us goes against the grain. We feel comfortable with our brains churning around past incidents and future plans. Casting off the mechanisms of thought and taking the leap into the great swimming pool of the present feels decidedly risky.

Listening to the inner voice

De Caussade suggests we can have thoughts about the past and future, as well as spontaneous intuitions occurring in the present, but we cannot have them *simultaneously*. He puts his faith in the intuitions. He believed that at any given moment it is possible to know what we should be doing.

He advised the nuns of Nancy that something would prompt them to talk or listen to a particular person, or perhaps read a certain book, or do some other action. In order to receive that prompt, we must consult 'our hearts' (what might now be called 'intuition'): 'We ought to listen attentively to the words uttered in the depths of our heart at every moment,' he said. By doing so we will receive divine guidance that bypasses 'sense and reason'.

But listening to our 'hearts' and carrying out what they instruct us to do is easy in theory but not in practice. Like learning to swim underwater, it is something we have to dive into and learn on the job. The only good thing is that we do not need to have specialist knowledge or expertise in order to do it; we don't have to study theology for five years or meditate on top of a mountain. Listening to our hearts (intuition), De

Caussade says, is something we can all do – it is a treasure 'offered to us at all times and in all places'.

To listen to our inner promptings in the present moment means we have to take one crucial step: self-surrender, or letting go of our controlling egos. To relinquish our sense of conscious control is difficult. It requires trust – that what will happen to us in our seemingly vulnerable state of self-surrender will be for the best, even if it looks doubtful at the time.

It is this trust (for De Caussade it was trust in God or divine providence) that gives us the confidence to surrender ourselves. If we do that, our souls become as 'light as a feather, liquid as water, simple as a child… in receiving and following all the inspirations of grace'.

If we can surrender ourselves to the promptings of our hearts, we will only have to deal with whatever comes up, moment by moment. Those things might be pleasant or unpleasant, comforting or unsettling, but whatever they are, we have to remain in the zone of abandonment. We will doubtless hear the chattering voice of the excluded ego suggesting alternatives to what we are doing, in which case we must always refer back to our hearts, or intuition.

The four images

De Caussade illustrates this devotion to the present moment, and how we must trust it and not worry about the bigger canvas of our lives, with four memorable images or scenarios, involving a tapestry, a statue, a printed book page and a traveller.

Firstly, he compares someone who is living moment by moment to a tapestry being created stitch by stitch. On the underside of the tapestry the stitches may look higgledy-piggledy, but when the tapestry is turned over onto its right side, the whole pattern can be seen in all its beauty. Likewise, during the course of our lives, we are aware only of our moment-by-moment actions (like the individual stitches), not of the end result. We have to trust that our lives will eventually be revealed to resemble a beautiful tapestry.

In a similar way, if a statue in the act of being carved could speak, it might admit that it does not understand what the sculptor is doing, but at the same time affirm that it has faith the sculptor knows what is best. Although each blow of the chisel may seem like an injury, the statue, as it were, relaxes into the present moment, surrendering to a process it believes will have a positive outcome.

Then De Caussade suggests that a divine author is writing a book in our hearts. Although we are aware of the individual words being inscribed, we cannot read the whole book until it is published on the day of judgment. We may indeed wonder what the words mean while we are alive, but we will remain puzzled. This, he says, is because: 'We are still in the dark night of faith. The paper is blacker than the ink, and there is great confusion in the type. It is written in characters of another world and there is no understanding it except in Heaven.'

As the stitches on the reverse side of the tapestry make no sense to us until 'the day of glory', so it is with the type. But, like the finished tapestry seen the right way up, our individual stories will be beautiful in their entirety.

Lastly, De Caussade says that we must have the same sort of faith as a traveller who, when journeying across fields at night in an unknown country, has to abandon himself to a guide. Once we have made up our minds that the guide is good and trustworthy, we simply have to let ourselves go and obey his orders.

He points out that there is something exciting and energizing about not having a spiritual map setting out our route. We have to jettison our knowledge from books and rely on guidance from the darkness. The unknown, because it is unpredictable, forces us to be spontaneous: '…divine action is ever fresh, it never retraces steps, but always marks out new ways… It acted in one way yesterday, today it acts differently.'

The present moment is a challenge, a commitment and an excitement. We can all live in it and to do so would doubtless revolutionize our existence. The first step, I believe, is to become aware of those things that stop us from living in the present – our desire to control events as much as possible, instead of letting them unfold and reacting to them accordingly, for example. Or our inability to let go of things that have passed.

After that, we have to take the plunge of self-surrender – of accepting what comes our way without complaint. The difficulty is to treat those things we dislike in the same way as those we enjoy. The way to do this, De Caussade would say, is to remind ourselves that everything is for the good, ultimately. We need to remember the stitches of the tapestry, the chiselling of the statue and being led in the dark by the guide. If we can do that, we may have enough trust to risk committing ourselves to the present.

DIOGENES: CULTIVATING THE INNER CYNIC

'If I hadn't been Alexander, I would have
liked to have been Diogenes.'

WORDS ATTRIBUTED TO ALEXANDER THE GREAT

'Cynical' is one of those words that instantly conjures up malicious intent: a cynical remark, a cynical tackle (in football, say), a cynical decision, a cynical character. It suggests being contemptuous of other people's apparently good motives, being sarcastic, mocking, calculating, cold-hearted. The Irish wit Oscar Wilde once quipped that a cynic was someone who knew 'the price of everything, and the value of nothing'.

Yet, cynicism isn't always easy to detect: my opinion that a politician is making rash promises in order to win votes may be cynical, but on the other hand it may be saying nothing more than the truth. Another Irish writer, George Bernard Shaw, said that what people call cynicism is often simply the 'power of accurate observation'.

Nevertheless, it is strange that 'cynic' originally referred to a respected tradition of ancient Greek philosophy. How did the ancient 'Cynic' become the modern 'cynic', and why are the ideals of the Cynics important for us today?

It is hard to loosen the negative associations from the word 'cynic', but it originally meant 'like a dog' (it comes from the Greek word *kuon*, 'dog'). In what way were the ancient Cynic thinkers like dogs? Aristotle said there were four reasons: 1) The Cynics lived rough; 2) They were shameless; 3) They were good guards (of their philosophy); 4) They knew the difference between friends and foes.

The founder of the Cynics was a man named Antisthenes, who was born in Athens in about 445BC and became known for upholding the philosophy's ideals of living ascetically and pursuing virtue rather than pleasure. He died in about 365BC and his Cynic successor was the most famous of them all – Diogenes, who is still highly regarded and influential among modern thinkers and artists. It is not clear whether the two men ever met, but Diogenes was certainly in Athens when the reputation of Antisthenes, if not the man himself, was strong.

Living rough

Unfortunately, Diogenes did not leave a body of writings that reveal his teachings, but his satirical and caustic wit, his pithy wisdom and the example of his strange lifestyle were preserved in the works of later writers, especially those of a man named

Diogenes Laertius (no relation), who lived more than 400 years after Diogenes's death.

The anecdotes told about Diogenes may have been embroidered over time, but they are consistent in showing that he was an eccentric character – a radical maverick who challenged the norms of society and everyone he considered pompous, proud, powerful and status-conscious.

Diogenes spoke few words, preferring to make his point through his actions. For example, he once lit up a lamp and took it with him through the city streets in broad daylight. When surprised onlookers asked him what he was doing, he replied that he was looking for a 'true human being'. There was definitely something of the performance artist about him. The words he did speak were witty and brutally honest and he hated humbug and pretentiousness.

Diogenes advocated a frugal lifestyle and practised what he preached. For a start, he lived in a barrel or tub (it was actually a large earthenware jar used to store rainwater, turned on its side) in Athens and Corinth for many years – almost analogous to a member of a homeless community living in a cardboard box in a modern city. The difference was that Diogenes inhabited his barrel out of choice. He wanted to live as simply and freely as possible – free, that is, from the restraints of society, government and the so-called material necessities of life.

He rejected the trappings of power, authority and wealth, and he aimed his barbs at those who embodied them. (Goodness knows what he would have said about the politicians, bankers, lawyers and other pillars of the modern Western establishment.) For example, he was once sunning himself beside his barrel in Corinth when he felt a shadow fall on his face. He looked up and saw Alexander the Great, King of Macedon, the most powerful man in the Western world. Alexander had heard about Diogenes and wanted to test his reputation for ascetic living. He told him to ask for anything he wanted and it would be granted.

Diogenes thought about it and said there was one thing the king could do for him. I can imagine the theatrical pause and the look on Alexander's face when Diogenes then said: 'Could you move, you're blocking the sunlight.' Alexander could see he had met his match in the 'Dog'.

From Sinope to Athens

Diogenes was born in about 412BC in Sinope, a Greek settlement on the Black Sea coast of what is now Turkey (the town still exists as Sinop). Not much is known about his early life, but it seems he and his father worked in the banking business and that at some point Diogenes was charged with defacing the coinage. It is not known whether this charge was politically motivated, but we do know that Diogenes left Sinope, possibly exiled as a punishment.

Diogenes travelled to central Greece and made his way to the sacred shrine of Delphi, set among mountains and the home of the famous oracle. There he consulted the pythia (a priestess who would fall into a trance and speak oracular utterances) about his life and was surprised to be told that he should 'deface the currency'.

Was this a bad-taste joke referring to his dealings with money in Sinope? Diogenes interpreted the answer as a metaphor: by 'deface the currency' the oracle was referring not to currency as in money, but to the social and political currency, or state of affairs, of his times. He now believed his goal in life was to 'deface' or criticize it.

Diogenes continued his journey through mainland Greece and arrived in Athens in about 370. He took up residence there and showed an interest in philosophy by attending the lectures of Plato, the star pupil of the great Socrates and the pre-eminent thinker of his day. But the man from Sinope was not impressed. Plato liked to discuss topics such as the nature of reality, the soul and the afterlife, and the structure of society, and this was far too abstract and theoretical for Diogenes. He declared Plato's lectures to be 'a waste of time' and joked about his obsession with words and meanings.

To make his point, on hearing that Plato had defined a human being as an animal that was 'two-legged and featherless', Diogenes plucked a chicken and carried it into Plato's lecture room with the words: 'Here's Plato's human being'. This, we are told, forced Plato to revise his definition to 'two-legged and featherless with broad nails'.

Diogenes also criticized Plato's decision to teach philosophy to Dionysius II, the ruler of the city of Syracuse on the island of Sicily, a patron far too rich and powerful for Diogenes's liking. One day, Plato saw Diogenes washing lettuces and told him that if he had been smarter and paid court to Dionysius he would not now be washing lettuces. Diogenes retorted: 'If you had washed lettuces, you wouldn't have paid court to Dionysius.' We don't know how Plato responded to Diogenes's point about the value of humility, but he did pay the Dog a back-handed compliment by calling him 'Socrates gone mad'.

Diogenes didn't just challenge the Alexanders and Platos of his world. By living on a street in Athens in his barrel (a dwelling apparently inspired by watching snails carry their homes on their backs), he came into contact with the full spectrum of Athenian life. In some ways he would have had a similar role to a medieval Christian hermit, living rough, begging for his food and being called on to dispense words of wisdom.

The big difference was that whereas hermits were rejecting society by living in wild places, Diogenes preferred to mingle with people, the better to give them feedback on their lifestyles. He would also have been impatient with prayer or other religious matters, since he wanted to focus on the here and now and the study of humankind.

The Dog stayed in Athens for about 20 years, chatting to all and sundry, giving advice to those who sought it (and to those who didn't!) and attracting the sneers of the rich and the intelligentsia. He tried to reduce his reliance on material things to the bare minimum. It is said he threw away his cup after he saw a child using his hands to drink water, and when he saw another child using bread as a makeshift plate to eat lentils, he threw away his bowl, too.

A slave in Corinth

In about 350BC, Diogenes's life took a dramatic turn. During a sea crossing to the island of Aegina, which lies about 30 km (19 miles) from Athens, the ship he was sailing on was captured by pirates, who carried him off to a slave market on the island of Crete.

If anyone's lifestyle had been a good preparation for slavery, it was Diogenes's. In the slave market he was spotted by a man from Corinth named Xeniades, who was evidently impressed by the Dog's strange boast that his chief gift as a slave was the ability to 'govern men'. It is to Xeniades's great credit that he saw in this eccentric character someone who might tutor his two sons. He bought Diogenes and took him back to Corinth.

Diogenes resided in Corinth for the rest of his life. He taught Xeniades's sons to use weapons, to ride horses and to hunt. He also made them learn poetry and episodes of history by heart – evidence that, despite his stripped-down lifestyle, he was an educated and talented man. Furthermore, he showed them how to live modestly and to subsist on plain food and water. Some say that Xeniades freed Diogenes, or that the Dog gained his freedom after his master's death. When this occurred, Diogenes was too settled in Corinth to leave the city. Instead, he shifted residence to a barrel situated just outside the city's gates.

He did not stay in his barrel day in, day out, though. He would wander the streets and sometimes attended public gatherings, such as festivals of games, where he would mingle with the crowds and dispense his wisdom. On one occasion a proud athlete boasted to him that he had just won a foot-race and was the fastest man on Earth. 'So what,' Diogenes said. 'In the world of ants one of them probably moves faster than the rest. Do you think they admire that?'

A nagging conscience

Diogenes died in Corinth in 323BC, the same year that Alexander the Great passed away. Some reports say he died by holding his breath, from eating raw octopus or, more appropriately, from a dog bite. Perhaps it was simply old age. According to one story, he was buried beside one of Corinth's gates, commemorated by a marble dog set on a column on top of his grave. Later, a bronze statue was added with the inscription: 'Time makes even bronze grow old: but your glory, Diogenes, all eternity will never destroy.'

How can Diogenes help us today? Through the example of his words, actions and lifestyle. His mission was to deface the currency of society – that is, to point out its abuses and injustices – and the stupidity of various customs, regulations and laws – and also to criticize those who benefited from or who were implicated in creating its corrupt nature. He once said that he disliked wicked people for their wrongdoings and virtuous people for keeping quiet about them – a state of affairs that still prevails.

In other words, Diogenes was the nagging conscience of the people of Athens and, later, Corinth. He lived like a dog – homeless, eating scraps, and barking at the rich, proud, famous and self-satisfied. He was like a distorting mirror, showing the absurd or ugly contours of those who dared to stare at him.

A later writer named Maximus of Tyre recorded that Diogenes cut away all that was unnecessary in his life, 'liberating his spirit from the chains that had once bound him'. He lived 'like a bird, an itinerant, free', unconstrained by state laws and marriage and children (when asked the best time for a man to marry, he replied: 'For a youth, not yet: for an old man, never.').

He feared 'neither governments nor tyrants'. The idea of serving in the army was completely alien to him, and indeed he rejected any sort of nationalistic sentiment or loyalty to a particular city-state. Instead, he called himself a 'cosmopolite': a citizen of the world. I can imagine that today, Diogenes would identify with eco-warriors, satirists, politically motivated stand-up comedians and performance artists, conscientious objectors, protesters and the like.

But along with his negative approach to what he regarded as 'bad living' (e.g. striving for power and riches), Diogenes also believed we must take life seriously and engage in whatever activities we choose to do with respect and wholeheartedness. According to Diogenes Laertius, the Dog thought that 'nothing in life has any chance of success without long, hard practice; and this can conquer anything'.

Jesters and Dadaists

The legacy of Diogenes can be seen in anyone who has tried to challenge complacency in individuals or groups, or has pricked pomposity. Medieval and Renaissance monarchs employed Cynic-like characters in the form of court jesters to amuse, but also to mock and criticize, the high and mighty. The seventeenth-century English diarist Samuel Pepys wrote that England's King Charles II had a jester named Thomas Killigrew who 'may with privilege revile or jeere any body, the greatest person, without offence, by the privilege of his place'. That is reminiscent of how Diogenes treated Alexander the Great.

The Cynic spirit can also be seen in the work of satirists. In 1729 the Irish writer Jonathan Swift published a tract in which he recommended that his countrymen eat their children, thus 'preventing the children of poor people in Ireland from being a burden to their parents or country'. Diogenes would have loved such a withering satire on the callous social and economic policies in the Ireland of Swift's day.

In the early twentieth century the Cynic tradition was embraced in the West by a group of individuals known as the Dadaists. They criticized the rigid and unjust cultural, social and political conditions of their day with a mixture of satire and debunking rhetoric. One of their founders, the German Hugo Ball, declared in the Dadaist manifesto: 'How does one achieve eternal bliss? By saying dada. How does one become famous? By saying dada... How can one get rid of everything that smacks of journalism, worms, everything nice and right, blinkered, moralistic, Europeanized, enervated? By saying dada. Dada is the world soul, dada is the pawnshop.'

The use of the nonsense word 'dada' to undermine what Hugo Ball saw as a 'blinkered, moralistic' society has the crackpot humour that Diogenes would have appreciated. The Dog would also have chuckled at the French Dadaist painter Marcel Duchamp, who once exhibited a reproduction of the *Mona Lisa* with a moustache and goatee beard drawn on her.

Duchamp was not being infantile (or not *only* infantile), but trying to point out that we are conditioned to view certain works of art in a certain way because of their fame, to the extent that we do not really 'see' the artwork at all but only our preconceived notion of it – 'It's famous so it must be beautiful.'

This is pure Diogenes: trying to get us to think for ourselves and to disregard the reputations of whatever is famous, whether people or things.

At a personal level, Diogenes can inspire us in various ways. His conviction that happiness has nothing to do with fame, power, pleasure and material possessions but with simple, disciplined living, for example, or his belief that we can become self-sufficient, steady in the face of the whims of fortune.

And his minimalist existence reminds us how complicated we in the twenty-first century have made our lives, with our myriad gadgets (TV remotes, dishwashers, security lights, electric blankets, extractor fans and so on), clutter (books, photos, paintings, ornaments, mirrors) and activities (yoga classes, meditation groups, book clubs, gardening societies). It is not that any of these things are bad, on the contrary; it is just that cumulatively they can make us forget what is essential in our lives.

Diogenes enjoyed sunlight and pure unpolluted air, a meagre amount of food and water, and fruitful encounters with his fellow citizens (however much he affected to be dismayed by other people and their values). That was about it. He seems to have been physically fit and full of energy and lived each day as it unfolded.

And his life wasn't easy. He was attacked verbally and physically by those he upset, which was just about everybody. No one who had status or riches or political ambitions liked to see Diogenes snarling from his barrel, or sunning himself on the street, apparently at ease with himself and ready to bark a witticism in the direction of anyone he felt needed taking down a peg or two.

It is said that some Roman emperors, when starring in triumphal parades in the streets of Rome after a glorious military victory, would have in their chariots a slave who would be told to whisper to them, 'Remember you are just a man', to keep their feet on the ground. Perhaps, in a similar vein, we should make it a priority to cultivate an inner Diogenes – a dog that barks loudly when we stray into moments of self-importance, pretentiousness, arrogance or smugness.

None of us likes to have those traits mirrored, yet to nurture a Diogenes voice that corrects our capacity to ignore our failings would be no bad thing. To indulge in true destructive cynicism can never be right, but to cultivate a witty, acerbic inner Cynic – a vigilant humbug detector – can only be to our benefit.

HILDEGARD OF BINGEN: GREEN ENERGY

'Who is this woman who rises out of the wilderness
like a column of smoke from burning spices?'

POPE EUGENIUS III, DESCRIBING HILDEGARD OF BINGEN

Feeling below par or mildly pessimistic, or lacking in energy, or being in the hinterland of depression are not, of course, new phenomena. But in the past it seems these types of low mood were often referred to as 'accidie' (pronounced 'acsidy'). Accidie was the condition that was said, for example, to afflict early Christian hermits living in the desert – a malevolent spirit that made them feel their lives were useless and prevented them from working or praying.

To live in the desert and dedicate yourself to God takes great willpower and discipline, not to mention faith, so accidie was the most insidious of conditions – it undermined the point of your existence. In the Middle Ages, accidie was even considered a sin. As the English poet Geoffrey Chaucer said in 'The Parson's Tale', accidie makes you 'hevy, thoghtful, and wraw', which might be translated as 'lethargic, self-absorbed and irritable'. Accidie took you away from your Christian life, imperilling your soul.

The word accidie seems to have faded away in the centuries after the Middle Ages, and it is rarely used today. But the emotion – perhaps something more like melancholy than depression, discontent with life rather than despair – has not gone away. In fact in Western culture, where ambition and the pleasure principle are strongly embedded, accidie often lurks and oozes out the moment some achievement has been attained, or the buzz of sensation has faded from the mind.

It brings with it a sense of restlessness and dissatisfaction with everything. It is similar to laziness (or the sin of sloth, as it was known), but is more a state of being, rather than isolated instances of not being bothered to do anything creative or productive. I may be too lazy to change from slippers to shoes to put the rubbish out in the rain, but accidie would stop me from going out at all.

When the insidious mist of accidie drapes itself around you, sucking out energy and making you feel like a lump of dough searching for a pinch of yeast, a good person to turn to as a corrective is the twelfth-century German nun Hildegard of Bingen. It may not always help: sometimes accidie has to be ridden out. You just have to lie low and let its disabling current of air waft over you. But the process might be short-circuited by imagining yourself in the guise of Hildegard.

The power of *viriditas*

It is hard to imagine Hildegard being beset by accidie. She may have been struck down with it at times, but her whole life was an embodiment of energy and creativity. There should be a single English word that describes these two qualities, something like 'creanergy'. As it happens, Hildegard did have a word that expressed them: the Latin word *viriditas*, which means 'greenness', but also the quality of being fruitful, abundant, fresh, vital, dynamic and life-giving.

Hildegard overflowed with *viriditas*. At the peak of her powers, she was running an abbey, supervising her nuns and giving pastoral care. At the same time she was writing books on theology and prophecy (based on the visions she regularly received), which she illustrated with beautiful illuminations. She also wrote books about the human body, the natural world and the medicinal properties of plants. She wrote musical compositions, too – songs and hymns still popular today.

She wrote letter after letter consoling, advising or haranguing nobles, abbots, popes and kings. And she went on tours, giving impassioned sermons to expectant crowds. She did all this while suffering from various illnesses, including debilitating headaches, which most modern scholars believe were migraines.

How was Hildegard filled with all this *viriditas*, this dynamic creativity? She herself ascribed it to a divine power that she called the *lux vivens*, the 'living light'. She received this force without willing it, by entering a different dimension of consciousness.

There were a good number of mystics in the medieval world, and most of them seemed to have revelations while in a state of rapture – when they were oblivious of everyday reality. Hildegard was notable for being able to receive powerful images while being fully aware of her surroundings. She wrote about experiencing the rapture of the living light, which would disperse her sufferings and melancholy, and rejuvenate her (she said it made her feel like 'a simple maiden rather than an old woman').

Scholars still debate the nature of Hildegard's visions, which were the source of her creativity. What is clear though, is that whatever the *lux vivens* was, it inspired her life to an extraordinary degree. It is hard to think of someone else during (or even before or after) the medieval period with such versatile talent.

It would be wonderful to experience the 'living light' and to be filled with *viriditas*. Hildegard did not lay down any methods for receiving this divine energy; it seems to have been a gift, peculiar to herself, and it may have been linked with the ferocious headaches she had (though, as scholars have pointed out, migraines do not usually lead to the sort of visions that Hildegard had and recorded). Yet the implication is there, I think, that we can all partake of the *lux vivens*.

What Hildegard had in her life to a greater degree than we probably have in ours was time, stillness, quietness and faith. It is these qualities, I believe, allied with a natural psychic gift, that allowed her to access the divine light. Perhaps we can access it too, with the right sort of stillness and faith. If not, the very example of Hildegard's life – just savouring her achievements – is a tonic to counteract lethargy.

As well as being multi-talented, Hildegard was also courageous. A woman born in the Middle Ages was expected to know her (lowly) place in society. The Church, all-powerful at this time, regarded women as second-class citizens, as did the secular world. The idea that Eve was to blame for the 'fall of man' from paradise was deeply ingrained, and there was a deep-rooted strain of anti-female asceticism in Christianity.

Monks and hermits traditionally prized celibacy and rejected the pleasures of the flesh (or were supposed to!), especially those involving women, who often became demonized. The English historian R.W. Southern said that for the Cistercian monk Bernard of Clairvaux, every woman was 'a threat to his chastity'. This pervasive attitude could turn to open misogyny.

But Hildegard managed to buck this trend. Caring little for St Paul's warning that women should be silent in church, she voiced her disgust, in sermons and letters, of Church corruption. And she wrote to the most powerful rulers of Europe, giving them the benefit of her opinions.

Community life

How did Hildegard become the way she was? Born the tenth child of a noble family in the Rhineland in western Germany, she suffered poor health from an early age. When only eight years old, she was sent off by her parents into the permanent care of a nun named Jutta, who was also from a well-to-do family. Jutta was an anchoress (like Mother Julian of Norwich, see p.51) who lived in a cell attached to the men's Benedictine abbey of Disibodenberg (named after an obscure Irish monk named Disibod) in the diocese of Speyer.

Sending Hildegard away from home may seem like an act of callousness by her parents, but it was not unusual for the time, and Jutta seems to have been a distant relation, someone who could be trusted to look after the young girl. Jutta effectively became Hildegard's parent, tutor and spiritual mentor, and guided her to become a fully-fledged nun at the age of 15.

As more young women joined Jutta, the group became a distinct religious community in its own right. In this way Disibodenberg evolved into a 'double monastery' – that is for both men and women, but with each group living separately. Hildegard and her sisters would have spent their days copying books, weaving garments, carrying out manual work, reading the scriptures and praying and worshipping. Hildegard must have shown herself to be especially devout and trustworthy, because when Jutta died in 1136, she took over as head of the community. She was 38 years old.

Hildegard's life changed outwardly with her extra responsibilities, and it changed inwardly, too, after she had a profound mystical experience in 1141. She saw the heavens open, and a flaming light burst out and filled her head and chest with an extraordinary warmth. This experience gave her insights into the meaning of the scriptures, and from then on she felt the need to write down the visions she received.

At first she was not certain of the status or value of her visions, but she confided in a monk named Volmar, who was convinced they came from a divine source. Eventually, Hildegard got approval for her visions from Pope Eugenius III and the Cistercian monk Bernard of Clairvaux, probably the most influential churchman of his time. No one was going to argue with those two! With their endorsement, Hildegard was able to receive visions openly and without fear of criticism, and to record her prophecies in books.

A new monastery

Over the years, Hildegard's reputation as a dynamic, wise and visionary abbess spread, and more women came to join her community at Disibodenberg. By 1147 a shortage of living space had become such an issue that Hildegard founded a new convent at nearby Rupertsberg, which lies on a hill just across the River Nahe from the town of Bingen. (She would establish another monastery in Bingen itself about 20 years later, and the modern abbey of Bingen was founded on this site in 1907.)

The Disibodenberg monks were unhappy about the nuns leaving, knowing their own lustre would fade with the absence of the now-famous Hildegard. One of the monks, a Brother Arnold, was particularly opposed to the move. But when a mysterious illness caused his tongue to swell so much he 'could not close his mouth', he relented; his change of heart coincided with a swift recovery of his health. He then helped to prepare the site for the new convent, clearing away vines with his own hands.

For the next 32 years, Hildegard looked after her nuns at Rupertsberg, wrote her books and letters (almost 400 of the latter survive) and composed music. In her letters she advised and warned the leaders of Europe, including Henry II of England and Conrad III of Germany. She was frank and fearless, telling the octogenarian pope, Anastasius IV, that he was too tired to do his job and too indulgent to his entourage, who she claimed were malicious and depraved.

Her letters also show a more personal, intimate side. When one of her nuns, a young noblewoman named Richardis von Stade, decided to leave Rupertsberg, Hildegard was distraught. She clearly felt a strong bond with her protégée and tried everything to stop her from leaving, but to no avail. Her letter to Richardis shows the depth of her feeling: 'Now, let all who have grief like mine mourn with me, all who, in the love of God, have had such great love in their hearts and minds for a person – as I had for you – but who was snatched away from them in an instant, as you were from me.' Richardis left to become abbess of another monastery.

As well as books on theology and prophecy, Hildegard wrote a nine-volume work on natural history called *Physica*, which dealt with seas, rivers, trees, stones and gems, and named nearly 1,000 different animals and plants. There was also *Causae et Curae*, a book that explored the causes of diseases and their cures. Hildegard had worked in the sick bay of Disibodenberg and would have had the chance to study the effects of animal and herbal remedies firsthand. Suggested remedies included sturgeon's bladder (for 'dropsy' or oedema – excessive fluid under the skin) and turbot's liver for eye problems. Primrose and fennel, she suggested, are good for melancholy, and arnica and lampreys for the libido.

If Hildegard was down-to-earth in her nature and medicinal writings, she was truly celestial when composing songs. More than 70 of her creations (collectively known as the *Symphonia*) survive and have brought her more fame – because of modern recordings of them – than any other aspect of her life and work.

She wrote her songs for monastic worship, and they include antiphons, hymns and responsories – songs for worship that were believed to reflect the celestial music that Adam would have heard before his and Eve's expulsion from Eden. Claiming she received her songs simply by listening to celestial voices, she worked in the tradition of the Gregorian chant, but her melodies are more varied and her Latin lyrics freer in structure.

Receiving the divine light

Underlying all of Hildegard's creativity and moral authority were her visions and her experience of the divine light, which she once described as being brighter than a 'sunstruck cloud'. This was the wellspring of her various talents and it gave her the insight to understand the scriptures, human behaviour and other matters. As previously mentioned, she could see her visions at the same time as being able to see the everyday world. It is hard for us to imagine how she could do this. It must have been similar to wearing bifocals – being able to switch from one sphere of clarity to another.

The images she saw tended to be larger-than-life and symbolic. For example, she saw the figure of a woman dressed in a white silk dress and wearing a jewel-encrusted cloak and sandals. She knew, or heard through a divine voice, that the figure represented 'Ecclesia', the Greek word for 'church'. She also saw that Ecclesia's clothes were dirty and torn and knew this symbolized the corruption of priests.

Hildegard engaged in a long process with her visions, writing them down (by dictating them to Volmar) and amplifying them with illuminated paintings (it is thought she probably provided the designs, rather than sat down herself with a paintbrush in her hand). Her best-known visionary work is called *Scivias* (short for *Scito vias Domini*, 'Know the ways of the Lord').

The book has a cosmic, visionary style similar to that of the Bible's Book of Revelation. Mother Church, for example, is illustrated as a crowned woman (so far, so good!), but then the eye travels down to see the shocking sight of a monstrous, bristly, snarling head (representing the anti-Christ) planted in her groin.

Elsewhere in *Scivias*, Satan and his angels are shown as a dramatic host of black stars that become cinders as they fall from heaven. And, on a more serene note, in another picture the Trinity is depicted as a man made of luminous sapphire surrounded by golden fire and a glowing light.

Throughout *Scivias* and Hildegard's other works and musical compositions flow the currents of *viriditas*. In her songs, she says that after God's creation of the universe, this 'greenness' eventually fell away from the world, but that through the power of the holy spirit, the Earth is made green again. In one hymn she compares the Virgin Mary to the 'greenest branch' of a tree, giving bloom to the flower of Christ.

In another Latin piece, beginning *O nobilissima viriditas*, she praises *viriditas* directly:

O highest power of green
Rooted in the sun
Shining in peaceful brilliance
Within a sphere beyond the ken
Of human excellence.

You are enfolded by sacred mysteries.
You redden like the dawn
And burn with flames of sun.

It is not surprising that ecological groups have picked up on Hildegard's *viriditas*, with its core idea of Earth's fruitfulness coming from a divine, green, source.

It is *viriditas*, too, that can make us better able to resist or overcome the condition of accidie described earlier. Perhaps because it carries the exoticness of the Latin language, the actual word *viriditas* seems to have an imaginative potency (perhaps, too, its echo of 'virile') that captures the essence of greenness and the energy it radiates.

It conjures up the green of the jungle canopy; the green of a well-watered lawn; the lime-green of new buds appearing on oak trees; the large green teardrops of chestnut tree leaves; the concentrated green of moss on stone; the green tresses of weeds swept forwards in a stream; water-meadows; the darker green of clover; the spiky green of chives.

We tend to think of colours as passive things, qualities we look at. But *viriditas* has an active force; it shines with divine splendour and burns like the sun. Through her life and works, Hildegard suggests that it is something that can change us, if we can allow ourselves to play with it imaginatively in our minds, letting its potency seep into our souls.

BOETHIUS: HOSTAGE TO FORTUNE

'Why did my friends harp on about my luck?
I stood on shaky ground: I came unstuck.'

BOETHIUS

Most of us like to think we are, by and large, rational, logical and reasonable in the way we behave and think. But is this really so? There are people who dread having good luck because they believe in a sort of law of balances: a stroke of good fortune will inevitably lead, they think, to a slice of bad luck to even things out – even though there is no cause and effect involved with good and bad luck. Good luck might follow good luck, and the same with bad luck.

The idea of fortune, of our lives changing swiftly from good to bad, or vice versa, has haunted humankind for thousands of years. The observation that a freak storm or a spell of hot dry weather could destroy a harvest and create a famine must have been a strong motive for engaging in prayer and ritual.

Because for as long as our ancestors experienced 'the slings and arrows of outrageous fortune' – a woman dying in childbirth, an innocuous sneeze leading to pneumonia and death, a storm at sea wrecking a ship – they tried to influence the mysterious forces of the gods, God or nature, which they believed controlled the events of the universe. Their main method was prayer and ritual (sometimes involving sacrifice) aimed at a supernatural being.

Yet there were clearly times when prayer and ritual did not seem to work. The Book of Job in the Old Testament questions the nature of bad fortune – why would God allow suffering to happen? Job is tested by a series of personal calamities. His friends believe he must have sinned to have incurred such terrible misfortunes, which they see as a punishment from God, but Job is adamant he has done nothing morally wrong. In the end, God settles the issue by telling Job that it is simply not his right to question His power, and Job repents in 'dust and ashes'. In effect, God pulls rank, and the mystery of ill fortune and suffering remains unclear.

Superstition and fortune

We may believe it is impossible to change our fortune (despite the words of the famous golfer who said, 'The more I practise, the luckier I get.'). It is hard to imagine our silent or whispered thoughts overcoming the traffic jam that is making us late for an important appointment. Nevertheless, many of us do try to influence fortune, often by performing rituals deemed to be 'superstitious'.

Sportspeople are known for wearing 'lucky' boots, coming out last onto the pitch, listening to a certain song before a game, not shaving and not putting on the number 13 shirt. Actors are not supposed to utter the name of Shakespeare's play *Macbeth* – to do so incurs bad luck – and refer to it as the 'Scottish Play'. To wish a fellow actor good luck before he or she goes on stage is also taboo, and the phrase 'break a leg' is used instead.

I am not sure of the psychology of performing superstitious rituals. I can understand a devout believer in God praying or lighting a candle to try to bring good fortune, especially since prayers and candles are full of positive symbolism. But stopping shaving or avoiding cracks in the pavement seem arbitrary. Which does not make them any less important to those who believe in them. Perhaps these actions are the equivalent of a tennis player bouncing the ball a few times before serving – they are designed to soothe the mind and create a rhythm.

The ancients were fascinated by the whole idea of fortune. The Greeks and the Romans had sacred sites where people could consult oracles – their equivalent to modern-day readings of palms, crystal balls or Tarot cards, or of the *I-Ching*, an ancient Chinese book of wise sayings. The most famous of the oracle shrines was Delphi in central Greece. A person would come along and ask a question about, say, who to marry or where to live and an answer (usually rather cryptic) would be given by a priestess inspired by the god Apollo.

For the Romans, fortune took the form of a goddess named Fortuna. She was the daughter of Jupiter and known for her capacity to bring both good and bad luck. Temples were built for her in Rome, and a huge cult centre was established at what is now Palestrina, about 30 km (19 miles) east of Rome. There, Fortuna's oracle consisted of a box containing oak strips inscribed with mysterious sayings. Visitors would come along with a question and a young boy was sent off to pick out one of the strips at random. The questioner then interpreted the words as best he could.

Boethius and the *Consolation of Philosophy*

The figure of Fortune survived into the Middle Ages, mainly through the writings of the late Roman thinker and statesman Boethius, who did much to popularize the image of Fortune's wheel – the idea that luck was like a turning wheel, always changing from bad to good to bad and so on.

In his book *Consolation of Philosophy* (which became a medieval bestseller and was translated by the English monarchs Alfred the Great and Queen Elizabeth I among others), Boethius reflects deeply on the best way of coping with these changes of luck. After all, he himself experienced huge changes in fortune, as we will see. One moment he was the most powerful person in the government, the next he was on death row.

Boethius experienced Fortune's wheel from early childhood. He was surely lucky to have been born into an upper-class family in Rome, but not so fortunate that his birth year was AD 480, a time of great political turbulence and social anxiety. Only four years previously, the fall of the western Roman Empire (the empire at this point was divided into two halves, west and east) had been sealed when the last of the emperors had been deposed by a military commander.

Boethius was unlucky that his parents both died while he was young, but fortunate that he was adopted by a man named Symmachus, one of Rome's richest and most cultured citizens. Thanks to Symmachus, Boethius enjoyed the best education possible, becoming fluent in Greek and learned in philosophy. Later, Symmachus allowed Boethius to marry his daughter, Rusticiana, who bore him two sons.

In 493, when Boethius was 13, Theodoric the Great, king of the 'barbarian' Ostrogoths, became the new ruler of Italy and the remains of the western Roman Empire. Theodoric was shrewd enough to recruit his government ministers from among the old Roman aristocrats, who were well versed in running the affairs of state. Would Boethius's fortune change again?

Eventually, when he became a young man, Boethius impressed Theodoric with his intelligence and honesty to the extent that the king commissioned him to work on a number of state projects. These ranged from investigating the debasement of Roman coinage to making a water-clock and a sundial as gifts for a neighbouring king. Boethius became increasingly indispensable to Theodoric, who, in 510, made him consul of Rome, the highest political office available.

But Boethius was not really a political animal. His great passion was for intellectual inquiry. He studied and wrote treatises on mathematics, geometry, astronomy and music, and was instrumental in making these subjects the basis of the medieval education system. He also set himself the gargantuan task of translating the complete works of Plato and Aristotle into Latin – and writing commentaries on them. It was a project he never finished.

Boethius's star continued to rise until he was in his early forties. In about 522 he reached the high point of his life and career when Theodoric appointed him Master of Offices, a highly influential court position, and also made Boethius's two sons joint consuls – an extraordinary honour both for them and their father. Running Rome had almost become a family business.

Yet, within a year or so, Boethius's world came crashing down. The king accused him of treason. It is not clear exactly what happened, but a Roman colleague of Boethius's named Albinus was caught writing letters disloyal to the king. By this time Theodoric was old, paranoid and prone to terrible fits of anger. He was incensed when Boethius tried to defend Albinus and had him thrown into prison in what is now Pavia, near

Milan. Boethius was denied the chance to defend himself in person against the charge of treason brought against him and was now effectively on death row.

It is unlikely that Boethius was confined to a windowless dungeon. He may have had a few creature comforts and access to some books. But even if his immediate surroundings were relatively humane, the spectre of death must have loomed over him. Nevertheless, he managed to write his *Consolation of Philosophy* while in prison. As it turned out, he was eventually executed in about 526. One source says he was tortured and then clubbed to death, another that he was, more mercifully, dispatched with a sword.

Fortune's wheel had one last turn for Boethius after his death. He was buried in Pavia and came to be worshipped informally as a saint under the name Severinus (one of his middle names). In 1883 the Roman Catholic Church formally approved his cult.

The wisdom of Philosophy

The *Consolation of Philosophy*, written under the shadow of execution, consists of a dialogue between the imprisoned Boethius and the personified figure of Philosophy, who takes the form of a woman and embodies wisdom and the light of reason. Together they discuss the nature of fortune, as well as fate and providence, and other matters. Boethius is clearly distressed by his incarceration and Philosophy tries to console him by making him look at his predicament from another, more enlightened, perspective.

For example Boethius complains about the lack of justice in a world supposed to be ordered by God. Philosophy reassures him that the universe is indeed divinely ordered and points to the harmony of the seasons as evidence: in autumn trees die and lose their leaves but their buds grow again in spring, and crops ripen in the summer sunshine; violets are ready to be picked in spring, grapes in the autumn; the sun rises and sets, the moon lights up the night. There is a rhythm to life that anyone can see.

So if the universe is ordered by God, why is it that good men are sometimes unfairly punished (like Boethius himself), and evil men prosper? One of the responses Philosophy gives is to make clear to Boethius the nature of Fortune, who hands out good and bad luck on a whim. The trick is not to invest in Fortune at all – to reject her value system. If you revel in the good luck Fortune brings (and in Boethius's case he had had great professional success), then it is only right, Philosophy says, that you have to put up with the negative things Fortune's wheel is bound to bring you.

The point that Philosophy makes is interesting: it is about neutralizing the power that Fortune holds over you, with her random mixture of goody bags and kicks in the shin, by reclaiming your own personal power. *You* decide how affected you will be by Fortune, not her. This does not mean to say that you have to be an emotional robot, unable to celebrate or mourn. But it does mean that you *keep a perspective*.

There is a sort of psychic equation here: the emotion with which you deal with success or good luck will equal that with which you receive a failure or bad luck. The more you exult in the former, the more you will be dismayed by the latter. But if when you receive success you remind yourself that it is relative, temporary, and that there are other more important things in life, then you will be better prepared for a disaster.

It is difficult to maintain this sense of perspective when you are plunged into a disaster because the instinct of self-pity ('Why me?' 'It's not fair!') kicks in immediately. So it is best to practice maintaining a healthy perspective when you receive *good luck*. The better you are able to see the place of good luck in the great scheme of things, the more likely you will do the same when bad luck comes along. This reminds me of two lines from Rudyard Kipling's poem 'If': 'If you can meet with Triumph and Disaster / And treat those two imposters just the same...'

Providence and fate

Another way that Philosophy addresses the problem of good people being afflicted with bad fortune, and bad people with good fortune, is to explain to Boethius the difference between providence and fate. Today, we often use the word 'providence' to explain a positive chance event.

For example, we might say, 'It was providential that my car broke down next to a garage.' We think of fate as being similar to providence but including good and bad events, with the suggestion that these cannot be avoided. As Shakespeare wrote: 'What fates impose, that men must needs abide; It boots not to resist both wind and tide.'

In ancient times, providence and fate had different associations, and Boethius explored the difference between them, trying also to relate them to the question of why good people sometimes suffer and bad people sometimes prosper.

First of all he took as a given that there is a God, and that this divine being has come up with a plan for everything that happens in the world. As an ideal blueprint inside the mind of God, the plan is called *providence*. When the plan is being put into operation in our everyday world of change it is called *fate*. So, there is one divine plan for all of us, and it has two names – providence and fate – depending on the point of view.

I think what Boethius meant is this: providence is responsible for everything that happens in the world and is concerned with the *overview*, while fate deals with the *details* of what happens to individual things. It is rather like providence being the president of a company – who has a strategic plan for all its different operations – while fate is the chief executive who implements the plan.

So, fate depends on providence: the chief executive (fate) cannot commence work until the overall plan of the president (providence) is known. Workers in the company might think some of the decisions being carried out by the chief executive (fate) are good one or bad ones, but what they are not aware of is the master plan conceived by the president (providence).

We can look at this another way by adapting one of the images used by Jean-Pierre Caussade (see p.81). A sculptor gazes at an uncut block of stone and imagines the shape of the woman's head he is going to create. He can picture her eyes, pointed nose, thin lips, high cheekbones, hair swept away from her forehead, and so on.

Having visualized the head, he begins to carry out the work, which will take a number of days. So, providence is like the sculptor imagining the stone block as a woman's head in its entirety; then, as he chips away at the stone, working out the best way to create the ideal effect, he is like fate, carrying out the detail of the plan.

Boethius said that providence knows what is best for us and we must accept it. It will not inflict adversity on those who cannot cope with it; on the other hand it might deal bad fortune to some people to stop them becoming complacent, or to toughen them up, or give them a glorious death so they gain posthumous fame.

Therefore, we should be wary of labelling certain actions 'good' or 'evil'. We only have partial knowledge and cannot see that events that appear to be evil are actually part of providence's plan. If we could see the whole ordered pattern we would refrain from calling certain actions and events evil. Therefore, when we think a good person has been afflicted by bad luck, or a bad person with good luck, we should realize that we don't really know what good or bad luck is, because we don't know the full picture.

Beyond fate

Boethius thought that the everyday happenings of our lives that we experience as fate are like a chain of events we cannot escape from. But he also thought that the closer we are to the divine realm of providence, the less we are affected by the bumpy ride fate gives us. Fate can operate only in our everyday world of time and change, where things live and die. Fate has no power in the eternal realm beyond time presided over by providence and God. Boethius seems to suggest that if we can reach a state of enlightenment (i.e. the timeless dimension of divine providence), we will remove ourselves from the remit of fate.

To illustrate this, he asks us to imagine a number of concentric circles nested within each other and all revolving around the same central point. The circle closest to the centre will be the smallest and move the least, while the circle farthest from the centre will be the largest and cover the greatest distance.

The still point at the centre is like divine providence, existing in a timeless realm. The circle revolving closest to it will be the one most able to share in its stillness and sense of timelessness. But the circle farthest away from the centre will be the one that is least aware of the influence of providence and may become tangled in the ups and downs of fate.

Boethius seems to be saying that when we get close to, or experience enlightenment, we are able to understand the meaning of the events that happen to us and no longer see them as the inexplicable dealings of fate. But if we remain on the outermost circle, we are farthest away from the still point and cannot understand the buffetings of fate that come our way. We feel as if we are bound by fate's chains (to use Boethius's own image).

Whenever we feel we are caught up in the stream of fate, unable to do anything but curse our bad luck or rejoice at our good fortune, it may give us a different perspective to think of Boethius in his prison, writing his book, baffled as to how he could have fallen from grace so spectacularly, and unsure of how many days he had left to live.

Good and bad fortune are inescapable; it is how we react to the whole concept of fortune and its changing nature that matters. By understanding fortune's fickleness, and by having faith that the seemingly random events of fate are in fact part of providence's plan for us, we can live our lives with a greater sense of security and serenity and be better able to deal with the daily trials we encounter. That is one of the lessons Boethius learned in his cell in Pavia, and which he passed on to us.

JALALUDDIN RUMI: EXPANDING OUR HEARTS

'Nothing but love can explain love and lovers!'

JALALUDDIN RUMI

'Love' is one of the most used words in the English language. In Western culture it saturates the lyrics of pop songs and is used liberally in poetry, philosophy and religion, from the Beatles' 'All you need is love' to the American poet Emily Dickinson's 'That Love is all there is, / Is all we know of Love', and St Paul's great paean to love in his letter to the Corinthians: 'Love is patient, love is kind. It does not envy, it does not boast, it is not proud...'

From an early age we are taught the importance of love. Children latch onto the word and demand verbal and other proof that their parents love them. We are told a child's sense of security is based on its feeling loved. Teenagers fall in and out of love, finding out that being 'in love' with someone is different to 'loving' them. The phrase 'in love' suggests the possibility of suddenly being 'not in love', whereas 'loving' implies less drama and immediacy but more constancy.

We know love is a good thing; we know that we should feel love (which traditionally resides in our 'hearts'), and we all want to receive it. We also realize it is a complex emotion. Sometimes we seem to be able to turn it on and off. You love your son, say, but when he's pulling the wings off insects you may feel your love for him being sorely tested. When he is consoling his younger sister you love him again. But when he's rude to your mother... Is love something that exists beyond temporary feelings of affection and repulsion?

Types of love

Some brave souls, such as the medieval churchman Bernard of Clairvaux and the modern writer and thinker C.S. Lewis, have tried to draw distinctions between different types of love. Bernard wrote about the four stages of love by which people came to love God:

- We start off selfishly loving just ourselves.
- We come to realize that life is difficult and that we need help from God, so we begin to love Him, but for selfish reasons.
- As we mature spiritually, we love God not just because He gives us comfort or solves our problems but actually for Himself.
- Finally, our love reaches the point when it unites us with God.

C.S. Lewis singled out four different types of love. The first three – affection, friendship and romantic love – are all what they sound like and are naturally available to human beings. The fourth type he called 'charity', a God-given love that enables us to love the unlovable (the sort of love that enabled St Francis of Assisi to embrace lepers).

Most of us do not think about love at all, let alone categorize it into four or more types. We tend to be conscious of love only when we feel it, or the lack of it. And it is easy to distrust our feelings about it. How often do people fall for someone romantically and think: 'This is love.' But when they fall out of love with the same person they are forced to wonder whether it really was love in the first place. Perhaps it was lust, or infatuation?

One writer who explored the subject of love in an original way was the medieval Sufi poet Jalaluddin Rumi (the Sufis were, and are, Muslims who favoured a mystical approach to God). Rumi wrote a lot about love, not in any systematic way but in scattered references throughout his voluminous works (his epic poem the *Mathnawi* is about the same length as Homer's *Iliad* and *Odyssey* combined).

Rumi's poetry and wisdom became increasingly well known in the West during the last decades of the twentieth century and by the time of the 800th anniversary of his birth in 2007 he was voted America's most popular poet – quite an achievement for a medieval mystic writing in Persian.

The holy man of Konya

Rumi was born in 1207 in Balkh in what is now Afghanistan, but which was then part of the Persian Empire. The empire came under the threat of the Mongolian warrior Genghis Khan and his vast army, who were advancing from the east, and so Rumi's family fled their home and eventually settled in the town of Konya in what is now western Turkey. In those days that area of Turkey was known as 'Rum' (pronounced 'Room') after the name 'Rome' (because it had once been part of the Roman Empire), and that is how Rumi got his name.

Rumi grew up in Konya as a devout Muslim and became a theologian and teacher, earning the loyalty of his students with his wisdom and charisma. Then, in 1244, when he was 37 years old, his life changed radically after a wandering holy man, or dervish, named Shams al-Din Tabrizi arrived in the town. Shams, it seems, had received a divine revelation in which he had been instructed to seek out Rumi. Now that revelation was fulfilled.

Not much is known about the mysterious Shams, but his effect on Rumi was electric. The two men seemed to be instant soul mates and were happy to talk about mysticism and related matters day and night, much to the intense jealousy of Rumi's followers. The pair were inseparable, until one day Shams suddenly left Konya, possibly, it is said, because he feared Rumi's querulous companions might harm him. He headed east to Damascus, leaving Rumi with a broken heart.

But all was not lost. Rumi sent his son to Syria to urge his friend to return. The son's eloquence was persuasive, and Shams came back. The two men carried on where they had left off, as if nothing had happened, once more engaging in long and deep conversations, and again inciting jealousy.

Finally, in December 1248, the two friends were separated again, this time permanently. One night, while Shams and Rumi were conversing, Shams walked out of the back door and disappeared for good (scholars speculate whether he was murdered by Rumi's jealous supporters).

Rumi was devastated. He searched for his friend, but to no avail. Instead, inspired by his feeling that he and Shams were 'two bodies with one soul', he wrote a long series of mystical poems in his friend's honour. He had felt the deepest love for his spiritual twin, and it is this firsthand experience that gives his poems such authenticity.

Rumi went on to have profound spiritual relationships with two other men, the second of whom, Husam Chelebi, inspired him to write his greatest work, the *Mathnawi*. For 12 years Rumi devoted himself to composing the book's 25,000 rhyming couplets. By the time he died in 1273, the poem was still incomplete, but it stands as a monument to mystical, or any sort of poetry. It has been called the Persian Qur'an.

After Rumi's death, the mystical Sufi order he had founded (known as the Mevlevi Order) continued to thrive under the leadership of his son. The Mevlevis still exist and are known as the 'whirling dervishes' for their cosmic dance (the *sama*), in which the dancer turns round and round in a fixed position while raising one hand up high and lowering the other towards the ground, symbolizing the role of human beings as intermediaries between heaven and Earth. The dance helps the dancer to reach a state of contemplation and even ecstasy.

Love explains love

Rumi's *Mathnawi* teems with wise sayings, quotes from the Qur'an, folktales, fables and parables. In it, Rumi typically illustrates profound ideas with simple stories or analogies. For example, in order to convey his belief that we are hampered by partial knowledge of the world, he recounts the traditional Indian story about an elephant that was put on show in a dark room.

People came in to find out what the animal was like but could not see anything. They groped around and touched the creature with their hands. One person grasped its trunk and said it was like a water pipe. One felt its ear and was convinced it was a fan. Another embraced its leg and said it was a pillar. And someone else touched its back and said the animal was like a great throne. Each person described the elephant in a different way. This is how we live our lives, Rumi suggests, unable to see the whole of anything because of our lack of vision.

What, then, does Rumi say about love, and what light does it shed on our experience of it? First of all, we should remember that Rumi was no dry theorist. He married, had children and was fortunate to have devoted friends. He experienced great intimacy with his trusted companions and it is plain from his writings that he experienced the sort of enlightenment that brought him into a loving relationship with God. He knew earthly love, and he knew ethereal love.

Rumi was wise enough not to try to sum up love neatly. He makes it clear that explaining the essence of love is impossible: love has to be *experienced*, and silence conveys it better than words: 'When we fall in love we are embarrassed by what we say about it. We can explain most things, but it's better not to explain love.' As for writing down a precise definition: 'Your pen might race away writing about this and that, but when it comes to love it splits into two...'

If words cannot convey love, then, what can? 'Nothing but love,' Rumi says, 'can explain love and lovers!' It's like trying to explain what the sun is to someone who has not seen it: 'Nothing but the sun can show you what the sun is. Shadows may indicate the sun's presence, but only the sun displays the light of life.'

For Rumi, love seems in some, if not all, cases to be a *cosmic energy* or force. For those of us who immediately associate 'love' with romance and affection this notion can be a bit of a jolt. In a way, it would be easier if English translations of Rumi used a word other than 'love', or kept the original Persian term, which is *eshq*.

But if Rumi does not explain what love *is*, he does, as a good poet, try to describe it, using a variety of images to conjure up the effect it has:

'Love makes the sea boil like water in a kettle.
Love crumbles the mountain into sand.
Love splits the sky with a hundred cracks.
Love heedlessly causes the Earth to tremble.'

It seems from these lines that Rumi is trying to get across the idea that love is a tremendous and universal natural power. It is not the love of a couple holding hands across a restaurant table on St Valentine's Day. It is something altogether more primeval and elemental.

In a similar vein, Rumi also says that 'Waves of Love turn the wheeling heavens: if it weren't for Love, the world would be frozen.' (This is a sentiment echoed by the medieval Italian poet Dante at the end of his epic poem *The Divine Comedy*, when he refers to 'the Love that moves the sun and the other stars.') These are big, universal images for something we usually think of as being small-scale and intimate. It is hard to imagine Rumi's love being fickle or transitory. It is more of a life force: something you fill your lungs or heart with – a vitalizing spirit.

As well as being a powerful cosmic energy, love acts as a reminder about some great loss in our lives. Loss of what? Loss of God or the divine home from which, Rumi believed, we all come. It is love, he says, that prompts us to remember and hanker for this lost state of divine existence.

He illustrates this loss at the start of the *Mathnawi* with the image of a reed flute (his favourite instrument). In the poem Rumi tells the reader to listen to the reed flute's complaint of being banished from the river bank from which it originally came: 'Ever since they ripped me from the bed of reeds, my haunting notes have moved the hearts of men and women.'

The flute's longing to return home among the reeds is inspired, we are told, by 'the fire of love' – again a phrase that conjures up energy and power. And as with the case of the flute, so it is the fire of love that inspires our own longing to return to God, the sole source of our ultimate happiness.

So far, Rumi's love has been both a cosmic force and a reminder of the loss of our divine home. He goes on to say that another aspect of love is that it transforms us in a positive, liberating way. For this to happen we have to play our part by recognizing our ego-driven faults and addressing them. By doing this we allow the power of love to flow into us and change us radically. Rumi describes this process with poetic images:

'Through love, that which is bitter becomes sweet;
Pieces of copper become golden;
Murky dregs become clear;
Pains become healed;
The dead are made living.
The king becomes a slave.'

The alchemy of love can create a world in which negatives are turned into positives and expected values and situations are reversed.

The lover and the Beloved

Rumi elaborates on the way we obstruct the influx of love with our egos when he writes about the 'lover and the Beloved' – that is the relationship between a human being (lover) and the divine (Beloved). Rumi says we block the path that leads us to the Beloved with our partial knowledge, pride, jealousy, anger, and so on. When we are truly joined with the Beloved (the divine), we are no longer aware of the separation between ourselves and it. But to achieve this is virtually impossible if we strengthen our egos by puffing ourselves up or being too selfish or ambitious.

The love Rumi speaks of propels us towards the divine, but at the same time it brings the divine towards us. It makes us and God equal partners: 'The sound of clapping cannot come from one of your hands without the help of the other one. The thirsty man may moan "O, delicious water!" But the water is also saying "Where is the water-drinker?" In other words, we (the thirsty man) and God (the water) form a two-way relationship.

I like this idea of mutual attraction, that love propels us towards God, and propels God towards us. It makes me think that on the more earthly level, romantic love between two people must also be reciprocal in order to be worthy of the name. If I fall madly in love with someone who is indifferent to my advances and emotions, can it really be love I am feeling? Or is it something more like an infatuation or a crush? The touchstone of love is surely that the depth of our feeling is mirrored by the person we love.

Rumi's notion of love – that it acts like a universal energy, makes us long for our lost, divine home and can radically transform us – does not, I think, replace the sort of love we have for partners, family and friends. Instead it accentuates or deepens our earthly love, making us more compassionate towards our loved ones. It can also enlarge us to the extent that we love those we would not usually feel charitable towards (in the manner of C.S. Lewis's 'charity').

It's an attractive thought – that we can allow Rumi's cosmic force of love to flow through us and lead us towards the source of the divine, while at the same time it helps us to love our intimates, and even strangers, with more sympathy. Rumi believed everyone could experience this love. But we have to take the first step by coming to terms with the ego obstacles we put in the way of it.

WILLIAM BLAKE: SEEING THINGS AFRESH

'The eye altering, alters all.'

WILLIAM BLAKE

How do we perceive the world? If I see marks on a rock that I believe have been created by wind and rain, but which a member of Australia's Pitjantjatjara Aboriginal people believes were created by the spear points of an ancestral tribe, do we simply agree to differ – and would it matter? Do our different viewpoints affect the way we live our lives?

The way we perceive things is one of those issues philosophers have been chewing over for centuries, from Aristotle and the other Greek thinkers to the present. There was, for example, the eighteenth-century Irish philosopher Bishop George Berkeley, who believed (crudely speaking) that whenever we close our eyes the objects of the world dematerialize. How we perceive things, he would have said, has as much, or more, to do with the mind as what is 'outside' it.

We denizens of the West in the twenty-first century tend to take the common sense view that objects are constantly solid, whether we close our eyes or not. We are so used to thinking in a materialist way that it is hard to imagine the world differently. We rely on our senses to connect us to reality, and we are used to scientists measuring and analysing matter and making it more understandable to us.

Accustomed to a scientific world view, we tend to be sceptical, at the very least, of phenomena that fall outside the pale of science and the senses – for example, ghosts, fairies and spirits of all sorts. And many would go further and exclude the supernatural element in religion. For example, it is hard to square modern science's view of reality with the idea that a wafer and a cup of wine can be changed into the body and blood of Christ through a formula of words.

In the medieval world, belief in God was as certain as our belief that when we open a fridge a light will come on. But today, in many parts of the West, the assumption that there is no God is prevalent. (It is important to note, however, that there are still areas where religion and a belief in the supernatural prosper. For example, a survey carried out in the USA in 2008 revealed that more than 50 per cent of Americans believed in a guardian angel; that's roughly 150 million people.)

If we are convinced that the material world constitutes the sole reality, does it matter? The answer is probably yes, because such a world view can breed intolerance. Those who believe reason and science are humanity's greatest gift can feel exasperated and even aggressive towards those whose outlook on life does not embrace the laws of conventional science – those who swear by homeopathy, say, or reiki, or Bach flower remedies and other elements of alternative medicine.

And they can feel impatient with people who claim Jesus 'has entered' their lives, or who believe in angels. (And of course it should be said that religious people, especially those who hold fundamentalist beliefs, can often be intolerant too.)

Flights of imagination

A materialist world view may simply make us grow too one-dimensional in our outlook on life – to the detriment of our imagination. Imagination is a gift, a way of seeing that requires an open, receptive, sensitive and sympathetic mind. If we are unable to imagine perspectives other than our own, then we can become trapped in a mental cage of our own making, and our spirits (a word scientists would take issue with!) may shrivel and perish.

As the Elizabethan thinker Francis Bacon said: 'They are ill discoverers that think there is no land, when they can see nothing but sea.' This sentiment was echoed in the Victorian era by the theosophist Charles Leadbeater, who declared: 'It is one of the commonest of mistakes to consider that the limit of our power of perception is also the limit of all there is to perceive.'

Leadbeater said in plain words what his contemporary, the Irish poet W.B. Yeats, expressed in his poems and essays. Yeats was fascinated by mythical tales and folklore and regretted that the world in which he lived was appearing to lose its connection with the traditional associations of nature: 'Once every people in the world believed that trees were divine, and could take a human or grotesque shape and dance among the shadows; and that deer, and ravens and foxes, and wolves and bears, and clouds and pools… were not less divine and changeable.' The rainbow, he wrote, was the bent bow of a god, thunder was the sound of his chariot wheels; a flock of crows passing overhead was the dead 'hastening to their rest'.

Yeats describes a world view different to our own Western orthodox one, a more poetical one. But is it less real? Supposing someone believes that a flock of crows is the souls of the dead. Do we have the intellectual right to say they are wrong, whimsical or crazy? The question might be put simply as: 'How do we react to and how should we treat someone who has a world view different to our own?' Someone, for example, such as the English poet and artist William Blake, who greatly influenced Yeats and many other poets.

William Blake is probably best known today for writing the words of the hymn 'Jerusalem', which alludes to an old legend that Jesus visited England as a young lad, perhaps sailing there on the ship of his merchant uncle, Joseph of Arimathea. Blake was undoubtedly the strangest of the English

'Romantic' poets, who included Byron, Keats, Wordsworth and Coleridge.

A visionary who once claimed he saw the ghost of a flea, Blake hated any rules or conventions that stifled creativity. This even applied to his dress code: he and his wife would sunbathe nude in their garden, sometimes reciting Milton's *Paradise Lost* to each other (when, one day, a visitor called round, Blake cheerily shouted out 'Come in, it's only Adam and Eve, you know!').

The visionary Londoner

Born in 1757, the son of a hosier, Blake grew up in London, a city he loved and which provided the urban landscape of some of his poems. Even in childhood he experienced the striking visions that suggested he would follow a spiritual vocation: he did so through his poetry as well as his illustrations to them and other people's poems.

At the age of 14 Blake became an apprentice to an engraver for a period of seven years. This was the foundation for the profession he would practise throughout his life. By the age of 25 he felt established enough to marry; his bride, Catherine Boucher, became a devoted wife and an emotional anchor. Blake was not the easiest of men to live with: passionate, often rancorous, whole-hearted, non-conformist, moody – he would surely have tested the patience of a saint at times.

In 1789 Blake produced a book of poems called *Songs of Innocence*, which, along with the *Songs of Experience*, completed five years later, contains his finest short poems. The best known of these is probably 'The Tyger', which begins:

'Tyger! Tyger! burning bright
In the forests of the night,
What immortal hand or eye
Could frame thy fearful symmetry?'

Blake describes the tiger in such wondrous terms that he seems to question what sort of God could have created such a powerful, luminous creature. It is as if the tiger is bursting out of the world of imagination, pristine and shining; as if, in fact, it was the divine blueprint for all the tigers incarnated in the world.

In 1800 Blake left his beloved London to live on the Sussex coast at Felpham for three years. The reason for his departure was to work as an illustrator for a man named William Hayley. Although Blake rejoiced in the pleasures of the countryside, he became worn down by the tedium and frustration of hackwork. When he returned to London it was a relief for him to get back to writing his own poems and illustrating them, and this he did for the rest of his life. He died in 1827, his reputation yet to be established. It was W.B. Yeats, more than anyone, who installed Blake as a poet of the first rank.

The Age of Reason

Blake lived at a time when England and the rest of Europe were absorbing the effects of what historians now label the Enlightenment. For thousands of years before this epoch of history, people believed, as Yeats suggested, that the invisible was as rich in life as the visible. Hierarchies of angels existed in the ether, and fairies, trolls and the like resided in remote places. The Holy Ghost was a presence, not a dogma.

But the Enlightenment of the seventeenth and eighteenth centuries changed all that. Science, logic and reason were its three watchwords. Anything irrational or superstitious was spurned. If you could measure something scientifically, then it passed muster; if you couldn't then it was rejected. Even in the context of established religion, a demonstration of spiritual fervour could be labelled 'enthusiasm' – a word intended as scornful. The Anglican bishop Joseph Butler told the founder of Methodism, John Wesley, 'that pretending to extraordinary revelations and gifts of the Holy Spirit is a horrid thing – a very horrid thing!'

Of course this world view had many benefits. Medicine, chemistry and philosophy found a new lease of life. Witches were no longer burned at the stake. But the period marked the start of a sensibility that saw the world in a monolithic way – in a rational, reasonable way, to be precise. The divine creation, with all its thunder, hailstorms, rainbows, snow and plagues, was replaced by formulae and observations made with telescopes. With the disappearance of the divine vanished a general sense of the mysterious.

Now a world without mystery has many advantages – it means we can walk down the street without having to hop over the pavement cracks, swerve around ladders and look eagerly for a second magpie when we have seen a first. But an unmysterious world can lead to a sort of spiritual or imaginative claustrophobia.

Blake hated anything that denied the free flowing of imagination, the creative spirit and spiritual energy. For this reason he disliked religion, if only because it was organized and regimented. It is hard to characterize Blake's own beliefs. He was a Christian who viewed Jesus Christ as the fountain of imagination and love, but he disliked Church dogma and devised his own spiritual system, which he set out in long poems full of symbolism. He also thought that a pub was a more suitable place for Christian fellowship than a church.

He also did not like any interference in the relationship between himself and the divine, especially from 'Priests in black gowns… binding with briars my joys and desires.' Most of all, he railed against those who, as he saw it, wanted to impose the reason-based culture of the Enlightenment at the expense of the spiritual dimension – individuals such as the English scientist Sir Isaac Newton and the European intellectuals Voltaire and Jean-Jacques Rousseau. As he says in this poem:

'Mock on, mock on, Voltaire, Rousseau;

Mock on, mock on; 'tis all in vain!

You throw the sand against the wind,

And the wind blows it back again.

And every sand becomes a gem

Reflected in the beams divine;

Blown back they blind the mocking eye

But still in Israel's paths they shine...'

Voltaire and his fellow Enlightenment thinkers can mock all they like, he is saying, but their attempt to throw their rationalist sand defiantly against the wind – an element of divine creation – backfires and blinds them.

The image of the sand shows how Blake believed that things can be seen in two different ways. On the one hand, sand is an inert substance, its tiny particles reminiscent of the atoms beloved of scientists (Blake actually refers in the poem to the 'atoms of Democritus', an ancient Greek philosopher who put forwards a proto-atomic theory). But viewed from the divine perspective, the sand becomes like tiny jewels shining in the sun. So it all depends on how we see things, which in turn depends on the way we view reality.

The 'doors of perception'

From early childhood William Blake saw things differently – literally. It is said that when he was four he screamed in shock at seeing the face of God at his bedroom window. Some years later, while walking in Peckham in London, he saw 'a tree filled with angels, bright angelic wings bespangling every bough like stars'. On another occasion, in summer, he was watching haymakers in the fields when he saw angels walking among them. He claimed to have constant access to a supernatural reality, communing with spirits and angels who directed his work. 'I am under the direction of messengers from Heaven, daily and nightly,' he said.

Today, Blake would be said to be suffering from psychosis, or a similar condition. But mental illness should really be defined not by what you see, but how you cope with the world. Blake managed very well. That is not to say that he was not lonely, angry, frustrated and depressed at times. He felt the isolation of the artist and was out of kilter with the mood of the times. But he worked hard as a writer and engraver, had good friends and a loving marriage.

Blake knew that his capacity for seeing things invisible to other people was unusual, to say the least. Yet he gave the impression of being constantly frustrated that others did not possess his type of vision – one which made him certain there is a timeless divine reality that we can access through our everyday world. He conveys this through these lines:

'To see a World in a grain of sand,
And a Heaven in a wild flower,

Hold Infinity in the palm of your hand,

And Eternity in an hour.'

The lesson Blake teaches us today is that we must challenge our way of seeing the world in only one dimension. This does not mean that we have to pretend to see angels when we don't, but to look at trees, clouds, mountains, sea, rivers, flowers, roads, hedgerows, the faces of people not as cold, calculating rationalists but as individuals endowed with imagination, able to see deep down below the surfaces of things to detect their inner essence, and to celebrate their wonder. It's what most painters and other artists do as a matter of course.

Blake believed this gift of imagination, of visionary power, of seeing the holiness in things, was natural and open to everyone. Most of us are unaware of it, he said, because of the habitual and limited way we think and behave: 'If the doors of perception were cleansed everything would appear to man as it is, infinite. For man has closed himself up till he sees all things through narrow chinks of his cavern.'

Science is a wonderful discipline. A world without painkillers and anaesthetics, for example, is now unimaginable. But the scientific viewpoint, which sees the world as inert matter, infinitely explainable and without mystery, can be a dull place, or worse – a sort of grey limbo-land where a stifling spiritual-less miasma forces people into the escape routes of drink and drugs. Blake would encourage us to open our minds, or at least not close them. You don't have to see angels in the sun, but at least, he would entreat, do not shut off your minds from those who do.

LI BAI: FRIEND OF THE EARTH

'The scent of heaven is all round, divine music
Flows through the emptiness endlessly.'

LI BAI

Concern about ecological issues has become so commonplace in the West that it is almost as pervasive as the air we breathe or the stars in the sky, as long as we do not live where the air has a pollution haze and street lighting blots out the minutiae of the night. Global warming, deforestation, loss of animal species, over-fishing – the list reads like the specials menu in the Grim Reaper's bistro.

And then there are the world summits, global agreements and protocols. Just as it seems that hope and common sense are surfacing, we find countries not signing up to the agreements, scientists telling us that there is no hard evidence to back up fears about climate change, eco-warriors issuing dire warnings, and so on.

All of these issues can have an insidious effect on the way many of us think and feel. They form a backdrop to our daily lives, contributing an insistent tinge of pessimism (the world coming to an end sooner rather than later), a wash of melancholy (another species extinct), bursts of anger (city skyscrapers wasting electricity at night) and a sense of powerlessness (what can we do about it?). They form a thin miasma of fear, anxiety and impotent rage reminiscent of the atmosphere during the Cold War – an era of barely expressed but deep-seated anxiety over global destruction.

We also tend to think of ecological problems in terms of their effect on life in the *future*, rather than the present. My eco-aware alter ego thinks: 'Things are not great at the moment, but just about manageable; however, if we go on like this [chopping down forests, over-fishing, burning oil], what sort of a mess will our children or grandchildren be faced with?' It is the idea of our descendants inheriting the world as a desert or one huge swamp that alarms us. *We* will probably be just about all right (enough oil for another 60 years?), but as for our progeny…

It is my view that our understandable desire to safeguard the future is actually one of the problems of ecology awareness in the present. If, for example, you suspect that soot and creosote are building up in your chimney, you will make an appointment with the chimney sweep for tomorrow, or next week, or maybe in a month or two. But if your chimney actually catches fire you'll try to douse the flames, or phone the fire brigade immediately.

It is a similar scenario with the environment. We are concerned about it, but we do not feel any urgency to change our behaviour. Believing the world's oil is running out, we may make fewer car trips to town, but cutting down on petrol is not a radical change, it is simply a slowing down of the old system.

If you were told that in 15 weeks' time you would never have another drop of oil, what would you do? You might buy a bicycle, or a horse and take riding lessons; or you might try to move to a house near a town centre, install solar panels and a central heating system fuelled by wood pellets and buy a scythe to cut the grass. Your life would be transformed.

So, perhaps the most radical change we can make towards the environment and ecology is to change the way we perceive them in the first place. What is our true relationship with the natural world and its flora and fauna? What do we actually value about it? We often pay lip service to the idea of halting the extinction of species, or the disappearance of the rainforests, but how do we feel deep down about the endangered monk seal and the hump-backed dolphin? Is it a case of out of sight, out of mind?

Ruling the animals

We view nature through the lens of our conditioning. At one level there is family conditioning – for example, our parents might have instilled in us the principles of not killing creatures needlessly, or recycling materials, or not dropping litter. At another level there is cultural conditioning. We in the West have been fashioned by 2,000 years of Christianity – whether we like it or not – including its view of the relationship between people and nature.

There is a strong domineering side of Christianity when it comes to nature. This starts with the first Book of Genesis, which states: 'Be fruitful and increase in number; fill the Earth and subdue it. Rule over the fish of the sea and the birds of the air and over every living creature that moves on the ground.' *Subdue, rule.* That's hardly a motto for being harmonious with nature. Right from the start is the idea that nature is there simply to be used by people. It is easy to see how this attitude could have percolated down through the centuries to form an assumption about how we should treat the natural world.

Yet the situation is not so straightforward. Christianity also has positive views of nature – Psalm 104, for example, celebrates the harmony between its different parts. Water sustains the grass, which sustains the cattle and enables human beings to produce food; trees provide homes for birds, mountains for wild goats and rabbits. And Jesus, with his innate compassion, love of wild places and references to landscapes and animals in his parables and sermons, was clearly in harmony with nature.

Nevertheless, there is biblical authority for people to dominate nature. Also, over the centuries, the Church nurtured a tradition that beauty, whether artificial or natural, was a distraction from living a holy life. The story was told (admiringly) of how the great Cistercian monk Bernard of Clairvaux journeyed for a whole day beside Lake Geneva but in the evening, in Lausanne, showed no recollection of the glorious landscape. This spirit of the denial of beauty informed the Puritans and many other Protestant groups after the Reformation – the religious revolution that took place in the Western Church in the sixteenth century.

So there is more than one way in which we, as inheritors of the Christian tradition and its values, may have absorbed attitudes that distrust and devalue nature, or regard it as something purely for our own use. But how can we break free from them?

One way is to consider and reflect on how other religions relate to nature; perhaps we can learn from them and, if so, change our attitude towards our environment. What do Daoism (a Chinese religion that combines traditional 'folk' wisdom and rituals with various strands of philosophy) or Buddhism, for instance, have to say about nature?

The travelling poet

As it happens, there was a Chinese poet named Li Bai (also spelled Li Po) who absorbed both Daoist and Buddhist philosophy and wrote a lot about the landscapes he lived in and travelled through. His poems are reckoned to be among China's greatest pieces of literature – perhaps they can enlighten us too.

Li Bai was a colourful and complex character, a solitary individual who also loved conversation and drinking wine, a habitual traveller who was quite contented to stay in one place, a writer and thinker who liked nothing better than to sit with a blank mind, watching the trees shimmering in the wind or a river flowing through a deep canyon.

He was born in Central Asia in AD 701 and grew up to show great promise as a poet. He seemed to be destined for a safe, solid career in the Chinese civil service but he rejected it to pursue his poetry. By his late thirties he was an established writer and was travelling around China, committed to the life of a spiritual bohemian and artist.

He was a free spirit who drank from the current brew of Daoist and Buddhist ideas as much as from actual cups of wine. (It should be said that in Li Bai's day, Chinese poets believed wine helped inspiration by loosening the mind from too much conscious control.)

In 742 Li Bai was appointed court poet in the imperial capital of Chang'an, but he struggled to conform to his expected role. Two years later he was dismissed for his unpredictable behaviour. So he resumed his nomadic life, although it was made more difficult by his having to provide for a wife, son and daughter. His last years were scarred by poor health and civil war in the country. He died in 762. Legend has it that he met his end after rowing out into a lake in a state of inebriation. He saw the moon reflected in the water and leaned over the boat to embrace it, with fatal consequences.

Harmony with nature

Li Bai left behind a body of beautiful, luminous poems filled with his experience of nature, which was influenced by Daoist and Buddhist ideas. The poems illuminate what it feels like to be at one with nature, to be in harmony with one's immediate surroundings. For me they have the effect of opening up the mind and heart to a way of thinking and feeling radically different to the Christian view of nature.

To appreciate Li Bai's poems and his world view it must be borne in mind that for Buddhists and Daoists, nature was overwhelmingly a source of beauty and wonder. Daoists did not think of nature as having been created by a personal divine maker (unlike the Book of Genesis in the Bible). They believed that the different parts of nature (mountains, rivers, trees, flowers), which they called 'the ten thousand things', came into existence from a creative source of generation known as *wu*.

Buddhists (particularly of the Ch'an school, which became known as Zen in Japan) believed that by practising meditation you could reach a point where your mind 'disappeared', i.e. all your thoughts melted away until your mind was clear and still like a mirror, able to reflect nature – the ten thousand things –

with utmost clarity. In this type of 'no-mind' meditation – without any interference from thoughts, opinions, memories and the other contents of human consciousness – you could see the essence of the things of nature.

It would appear from Li Bai's poems that he reached this state of 'no-mind' meditation. In his lines of verse we encounter the 'ten thousand things' of wild China with exquisite clarity: orioles, crickets, 'howling gibbons', a black ox, a white crane and a Mongol falcon, as well as bamboo, deep-green moss, chrysanthemums, mulberry bushes, chestnuts, wisteria and willows. Everywhere the fragrance of pine trees fills the air, and mountains swathed in emerald-green mists, valleys, rivers and canyons give many of his poems a sense of great panoramic distances. Whatever he wrote about, he gave the impression that he felt at home with it.

In his four-line poem 'Mountain Dialogue', for example, Li Bai indicates an enviable harmony with nature:

'You ask why I've come to live in these green mountains;
I smile and stay silent, my mind contented, at rest.
Peach blossoms float off on the stream into mystery;
Here, with nobody around, it's another universe.'

The poem re-creates the actual experience of becoming one with oneself and with the external world. The first two lines suggest the process of meditation ('my mind contented, at rest') and set the reader up for the second two lines, where the perspective of nature seems to be from the point of view of 'no-mind'. By the end of the poem there is no 'I' to comment on nature – whether to love it, hate it or enjoy it.

In fact there is strong sense of there being no 'I' at all in the poem, and the result is an exquisite blending of the individual with the environment. The delicate peach blossoms on the stream symbolize how fragile and transient life is: in a state of mental harmony we can observe the blossoms – as we do the other things and events in the world – and let them go their way downstream, not pursuing what they are and where they are going.

Li Bai expresses the same sort of oneness with nature in another short poem, about visiting his friend Yüan Tan-Ch'iu, a fellow recluse, at his home on a mountain:

> My old friend living on the eastern mountain
> Loves the beauty of the hills and valleys.
> He lies asleep in the empty forest
> By the green spring, unwoken by the midday sun;
> Pine-scented winds riffle his clothes,
> The pebbly brook purifies his heart and ears.
> No noise, disturbance; I'd love to live like you,
> Propped up on a pillow of green cloud!

Li Bai describes his friend Yüan almost as if he has grown into his mountain home and become part of the flora. He is surrounded by trees and as he sleeps, the winds and the stream perform what seem to be cleansing or healing rituals on his mind and soul.

There is a stillness implicit in the landscape – the woods are empty, the sleeper is motionless, and even the movement of the wind and the water is gentle. This is a reminder of the stillness of Ch'an (Zen) meditation, when the 'I' evaporates. Li Bai writes as if without any interference of his 'self' or ego – until the very end of the poem, when he snaps out of his dreamlike evocation of the scene and expresses his desire to live like Yüan.

A good many of Li Bai's poems are similar to these two: descriptions of his relationship with nature that convey a strong sense of what it would be like to live in a world where nature is a friend, not a servant. What if we were to regard nature in the same way that Li Bai or another Daoist or Ch'an Buddhist did or does? Wouldn't it be that much more difficult to dump rubbish in a river, carve initials on a tree, pollute the air with fumes or deforest mountainsides?

When reading Li Bai and similar poets – Chinese or not – it is hard not to absorb their value systems regarding nature. One of the gifts of art is the way it changes the way we see ourselves and the world, and Li Bai does that with his exquisite verses. Through them we can recover our relationship with the world of nature, from the tiniest frog to the grandest mountain.

MARCUS AURELIUS: THE PRICE OF FAME

'The time when you forget all things is close,
as is the time when you will be forgotten by all.'

Marcus Aurelius

In 1968 the American painter and pop artist Andy Warhol was exhibiting his paintings at the Moderna Museet in Sweden's capital, Stockholm. In the exhibition catalogue he wrote: 'In the future, everyone will be world-famous for 15 minutes.' It is not entirely clear what he meant by these words, but at the time they seemed to reflect a world in which television and other media were able to propel unknown individuals into the world of fame in an instant.

In the 1990s and 2000s, the possibility of individuals becoming instantly famous was increased with the advent of the internet and social networking sites such as Facebook and Twitter, as well as the fashion for reality TV shows. Fame, once the preserve of the talented and the glamorous, the entertainers and the politicians, became available to almost everyone.

Fame is a curious creature. It is something a lot of people seem to desire, although they would probably deny it. We feel suspicious of it, but feel the allure of its glitter. The list of quotations about fame is endless, most of them negative and attributed to those who were already famous. Perhaps one of the laws of fame is that when you're not famous you want it, and when you are famous you feel obliged to say it is worthless, a nuisance.

The English poet Lord Byron, arguably the most glamorous and famous writer of the early nineteenth century, poured cold water on the notion of celebrity: 'What is fame?' he asked. 'The advantage of being known by people of whom you yourself know nothing, and for whom you care as little.' In the following century the American writer Truman Capote was equally dismissive, commenting that the only advantage of fame is that 'they will cash your cheque in a small town'. You can hear the note of disdain in their words, but Byron and Capote thrived on notoriety.

The fear of being a nobody

So, what is it about fame that attracts us? Why is it important for us to be seen on television and recognized in a supermarket? What does it add to our sense of self-esteem? I can see that for entertainers or sportspeople fame is a recognition of their popularity or talent, a validation of the hard work they've put in over the years. And I understand why would-be singers, actors and models would want fame because it's part of their business: by keeping themselves in the public eye they ensure they are invited to the right parties, premieres, chat shows and promotions, which in turn helps them to sustain their careers.

But it is more difficult to grasp why someone simply wants to appear on television or the radio, or have their picture in a newspaper, or see their name in print – regardless of whether he or she has talent or wants to make a career in the public eye.

It seems to me that fame has two prongs to its appeal. First, quite simply, it makes us feel important. The fear of being a nobody, and wanting to be a somebody, strikes at the heart of our vulnerable and insecure egos. As Napoleon said, in a brutally honest moment, glory may be fleeting, but 'obscurity is forever'. There is a part of us that craves recognition and, crucially, feels strengthened by it. It is a sentiment echoed by the English author Sir Walter Scott, who said: 'One crowded hour of glorious life / Is worth an age without a name.'

We build ourselves up on the favourable opinions of others, trying not to think of the possibility that the process can be reversed: our castles built from the sands of fame can be eclipsed by other, more impressive castles or washed away by a wave of negative or absent public opinion. 'Fame is fickle food upon a shifting plate,' wrote the American poet Emily Dickinson.

Second, I think we equate fame at some subliminal level with cheating death. Most of us are afraid of dying, and most of us want to be remembered for something. The hope is that after we depart this Earth, people will be sitting around admiring our paintings, books, deeds, and so on. Of course this idea begs many questions. For a start, when we die we might be totally oblivious of what is happening back on Earth. Yet, the idea of *legacy* – that our names and actions will continue after our decease – remains powerful and can become an obsession.

The wise emperor

Fame, and our need for it, therefore, could be a barometer of our sense of self-esteem and our view of death and mortality. This may seem like a modern preoccupation, but fame was much discussed in the ancient world, not least by Marcus Aurelius.

Who was Marcus Aurelius? It is a question he would have chuckled at, since he loved pointing out how well-known people soon became obscure after their deaths. Ironically, although Marcus Aurelius criticized fame, he was, during his lifetime, the most famous person in the Western world. That was the price you paid for being emperor of Rome.

Marcus Aurelius was born in AD121 to an aristocratic Roman family. His father died when he was young, but he was brought up by his grandfather and enjoyed a privileged childhood thanks to an array of talented tutors and the patronage of Emperor Hadrian, known not only for the wall he built in Britain but for being one of Rome's most enlightened rulers. Eventually, in 161, at the age of 40, Marcus became joint emperor with a man named Lucius Verus. When the latter died eight years later, Marcus was left as sole ruler of Rome.

During his reign, when he was not coping with famine, plagues and earthquakes, Marcus was mainly to be found directing military operations against hostile tribes threatening the borders of the empire. From Scotland to the Middle East, skirmishes, battles and full-scale wars were keeping the Roman legionaries on the go. Along the Rhine and Danube rivers the Romans fought off the likes of the exotically named Marcomanni, Iazyges, Suevi and Vandals. In 180, as he seemed to be winning the Danube campaign, Marcus died of an illness in Vindobona (now Vienna).

The *Meditations*

During his lifetime, Marcus was known as a just and wise ruler, as well as a military leader. But his posthumous reputation has rested mainly on a book he wrote, popularly known as the *Meditations*. It was a notebook, not intended for publication, that contained his thoughts – some of them scribbled down while he was on campaign – on the nature of fame, happiness, the brevity of life and many other topics.

Although most of Marcus's ideas can be traced to various currents of Roman thought of the time (particularly the Stoic philosophy), the eloquence and intensity of the *Meditations* are compelling. Down the centuries the book has fascinated thinkers, writers and leaders, including the eighteenth-century Prussian king Frederick the Great and former US president Bill Clinton.

The Stoic philosophers, who influenced Marcus, were the original stiff-upper-lip brigade. They emphasized the importance of self-reliance and being indifferent to whatever fate has in store for us. They were suspicious of frivolities and valued traditional Roman virtues such as honesty, integrity and truthfulness.

Marcus followed the Stoics' lead. In his book he tackles the craving for fame head on, looking at it from different angles and offering ideas and images to help us wean ourselves from its addictiveness. One approach is to remind us how insignificant people are, relatively speaking: 'Every person's time on Earth is short, and the place where he lives is small; even the longest posthumous fame is brief, and this is only continued by a succession of poor human beings, who will soon die, and who do not even know themselves, let alone anyone who died long ago.' This is a pretty bleak outlook for anyone cherishing the cosy thought of posthumous fame.

He drives this sombre thought home with the simple but rhythmically effective device of listing people who have passed away in succession:

'Lucilla buried Verus,

and then it was Lucilla's turn.

Secunda buried Maximus,

and then it was Secunda's turn.

Epitynchanus buried Diotimus,

and then it was Epitynchanus's turn.

Antoninus buried Faustina,

and then it was Antoninus's turn.'

And so it goes on.

There is a chilling lack of fuss (typical of the Stoics!) in this litany of mortality. Marcus makes the same point elsewhere by citing the example of four former Roman heroes – Camillus, Caeso, Volesus and Leonnatus – whose names would have been on everyone's lips in the days of the early Roman republic, but who, by Marcus's time, had long been forgotten. Today they are known only to Classical scholars.

In praise of not praising

Another antidote to our craving for fame, Marcus suggests, is to remind ourselves that human life is but a tiny point of time in history: 'The desire of fame may torment you, but see how soon everything is forgotten, and look at the chaos of infinite time on each side of the present, and the emptiness of applause...' If we can get a true perspective of our place in the universe, we can see how silly our need for fame is.

Marcus also thought that our fixation with fame is linked with our need for praise from other people (who, he remarked, probably lack judgment anyway). If we perform our tasks to the best of our ability, then no amount of praise will make us better people, or make us work harder. We need to be self-reliant, he said, and not become dependent on the opinions of others: 'Is such a thing as an emerald made worse than it was, if it is not praised? Or gold, ivory, purple, a lyre, a little knife, a flower, a shrub?'

From another angle, Marcus sees that the fertile soil that makes fame thrive on praise in the first place is our natural tendency to be impressed by appearances. If we can see things for what they *really are*, beneath the surface, we can make the soil less hospitable. For example, when we're eating something like pork or chicken, he says, we should imagine it as the ribs of a dead pig or the wing of a dead bird. Similarly, he points out that wine – a beverage that still attracts extravagant descriptions – is only juice squeezed from grapes. Likewise, a sumptuous purple robe is 'just a bit of sheep's wool dyed with the blood of a shell-fish'.

Clearly, it would be hard to maintain this sort of attitude: it is usually militant vegetarians who like to point out that a leg of lamb is a leg of a dead sheep. But Marcus was simply making a general point: that superficial appearances can beguile us and make us praise the surface not the substance. By getting into the habit of looking beneath the surface, we can appreciate fame and its fertilizer – praise – for what they really are.

Marcus's reductionist approach challenges the way we perceive things, especially ourselves: 'Very soon you will be ashes, or a skeleton, leaving behind just a name or not even that; but what is a name but only a sound and an echo?'

Happiness is a serene mind

Marcus does more than just chip away at our hankering for fame in life and after death. He constantly reminds himself, and us, what the point of life is – what we should be doing, what attitudes we should have, and how we should behave. His advice is characteristically solid, sober and unflamboyant: we should 'worship and praise the gods' (if we are good Romans!), do good deeds to people, speak the truth, be self-restrained and tolerant; and since we will always have to deal with events beyond our control, we should accept them gladly. It is a checklist of virtues that most religions would be happy to subscribe to.

Furthermore, Marcus goes beyond simply prescribing the do's and don'ts of good behaviour. He believed that the key to happiness is serenity and a well-ordered mind. We can achieve this by contemplation or self-reflection, he says – without needing a special place to do it in: 'People seek out external retreats such as country houses, sea-shores and mountains...

but it is up to you whenever you want to retreat into yourself.' A quiet room in an office, or a seat on a train or a bus is as good as a retreat centre in the country.

Marcus was also a great believer in people reflecting on their lives and finding their true vocation. He thought each of us has a guardian spirit or 'daimon' (not to be confused with 'demon'), a divine element that guides us to behave virtuously towards both the gods and people. He says that we should live according to our talents and vocation, just as people with specific jobs do: horse trainers train horses and gardeners grow vines, so we must concentrate on finding the right path for ourselves.

How do we know we are on the right path? Marcus prefers to ask: how do we know we are on the *wrong* path? One indication is a desire for fame, which is a symptom of 'dis-ease'. It is a sign that our values are wrong, that we fear death when we should be equable about it, that we rely on praise, when really the only happiness we can enjoy comes from serenity brought about by self-reflection.

Marcus's thoughts provide a sobering and compelling counterblast to our culture of celebrity and are all the more fascinating because they come from a Roman emperor, the most famous person of his day. They are not the bitter juice of the sour grapes of someone who always wanted to be famous but failed. Marcus was not only steeped in philosophy but had to deal with flatterers, sycophants, gold-diggers and the like all the time. He experienced firsthand the power of fame.

He is perhaps most helpful when he reminds us of our very small place in the grand scheme of things, and how petty our aspirations for fame really are: 'Look at it from a higher perspective: consider the countless herds of human beings and their innumerable rituals, and all their various voyages through stormy or calm weather; and all the different types of people who are born, live together and pass away.

'And reflect on the lives of our ancestors long ago and of our descendants in the future, and of the lives of foreign peoples: just think how many people do not even know your name, and of those who do, how many will quickly forget it. Reflect on the fact that those who might be praising you now will shortly be blaming you, and that your memory or fame or anything else is worthless.'

If that doesn't give us a sense of perspective of our standing in the world, nothing will.

ST FRANCIS DE SALES: VISUAL MEDITATION

'If you can manage it, meditate early in the morning, when the mind is not so busy and still fresh from a night's sleep.'

St Francis de Sales

Meditation has been practised for thousands of years, usually in a religious context. Those who meditate do so because they gain some benefit, such as feeling calmer, more peaceful or more alert. But it is also possible to have a life-changing experience through meditation.

That's what happened, after all, to an Indian prince named Gautama, who, after a long period of searching for the right way to live his life, meditated beneath a bodhi tree in northern India 2,500 years ago. He sat there for a few days before he suddenly found himself in a glorious state of enlightenment and became known as the Buddha ('Awakened One').

But if meditation is an essential practice in Buddhism and other religions, scientists have traditionally been suspicious of its alleged benefits, perhaps because of the religious overlay that it often carries with it. In recent years, however, scientific studies have shown that meditation can have demonstrably positive effects on people.

In an article in Britain's *Observer* newspaper in April 2011, the science writer Jo Marchant noted that trials at Exeter University in 2008 suggested that meditation 'was more effective than drug treatment in preventing relapse in patients with recurrent depression'.

She also reported that David Creswell of Carnegie Mellon University in Pittsburgh, USA, found that mindfulness meditation could strengthen the immune system and slow down the effects of HIV/AIDS, and that researchers studying meditators at a Buddhist retreat in Colorado came to the conclusion that meditating reinforces an enzyme in the brain known as telomerase, which is important for enabling the body to withstand heart disease, diabetes, depression and other conditions.

We live in a world of instant, and probably far too much, information. Google searches, emails, tweets and e-books bombard us with news, names, facts and figures like a meteor shower. It can be addictive: I can find myself checking up on a sports website every hour or so just in case some new, often trivial, information has been added.

Information has its place (it is convenient to be able to look up the weather forecast on the net, for example), but our minds need a rest from their relentless processing of the world's news. Quiet activities, from walking to knitting and gardening, are a positive way of slowing down our metabolisms; meditation proper – quite apart from the possible benefits listed above – helps to create calmness, insight and an emotional perspective that softens mood swings.

There are many types of meditation, and choosing one that suits you can take some time. Despite the wide choice, though, it is hard to go too wrong: simply sitting still and disengaging from everyday life, by watching your thoughts or repeating a phrase, helps to alleviate stress.

Some meditations emphasize being aware of the world around you; some are bound up with physical postures (yoga, for example); others require you to repeat a short phrase or mantra, or involve visualization (for example, of colours). One type of Buddhist meditation, known as 'mindfulness', involves cultivating awareness by carefully watching thoughts pass through the mind, like fish swimming in a river. The idea is to acknowledge but not get caught up in them.

In the West, Christians have had a strong tradition of meditation, although down the centuries it has been largely confined to monks and other committed believers and has usually focused on the mysteries of Christian doctrine. The closest that Christian meditation has got to 'mindfulness meditation' has been the practice of 'hesychasm', which developed in the Eastern Orthodox Church from early times.

'Hesychasm' means 'silence', 'stillness', or 'quietness', and was really a type of prayer that aimed to bring you into a state of inner peace, with the possibility of receiving divine grace. One aspect of it was the constant repetition of the 'Jesus prayer' ('Jesus Christ, Son of God, have mercy on me'), almost like a Buddhist-style mantra. In later medieval times, hesychasts recited the Jesus prayer in combination with certain breathing techniques and body postures, not dissimilar to yoga.

In Western Christianity, there arose a technical distinction between *contemplation* and meditation. Contemplation is more like what we would now think of as meditation: trying to create an inner stillness in order to move beyond the world of speech. 'Meditation', on the other hand, specifically meant studying a particular passage from the Bible or an aspect of Christian doctrine and reflecting on it in order to gain greater spiritual insight or warmth.

Over the centuries, Western Christians also developed a more visual type of meditation. In a way, the stained-glass windows and murals in churches and cathedrals in medieval times provided a means for visual meditation, presenting gospel stories to congregations who, in the main, could not read. Gazing at a depiction of Jesus on the cross could be as stirring as listening to a gospel passage about the same event. Also, the founder of the Jesuit Order, Ignatius Loyola (1491–1556), used visualization techniques in his *Spiritual Exercises*, which require the participant to imagine certain gospel scenes with great focus and intensity.

Devoted to God

Another pioneer of meditation was the French churchman St Francis de Sales (1567–1622). Francis was a persuasive advocate of visual meditation and the effect it can have. Of course, he was working within the Christian tradition (specifically Roman Catholic), and this might put off modern meditators unaligned with any particular religion. But what he said about meditation struck a chord with me, and I think his words, written in the early 1600s, are still applicable, to the spiritually or non-spiritually inclined alike.

Francis was born in Savoy, a small mountainous duchy wedged between France and Italy. The eldest of six boys, he grew up during a troubled period in France's history. Fighting between Catholics and Protestants (known as Huguenots) had begun in 1562 and dragged on until 1598. There was a 20-year respite before an even more bitter and wide-scale conflict, the Thirty Years' War, raged across Europe. (From these difficult times France was to emerge as the dominant country in the West, with Louis XIV, the Sun King, creating a court famous for its wealth and culture.)

Francis came from an aristocratic family and was educated at a Jesuit college in Paris. While there, he had a life-changing conversion experience. For a time he had been torturing himself with thoughts about the doctrine of predestination – the rather forbidding idea that from birth, people are destined to go either to hell (most people) or heaven (a small number of the 'elect').

A sensitive and impressionable young man, Francis became depressed, dreading the possibility that he would be among the ranks of the damned, roasting in hell. One day, in a fragile state of mind, he was praying to a statue of the Virgin Mary when suddenly his deep sense of unease lifted. He felt liberated, as if his mental burden had fallen away for good. From then on, he devoted himself to a life dedicated to God, convinced that everyone could be saved by God's love and not just the predestined elect.

From Paris, Francis went off to northeast Italy to study law at the University of Padua. After he had finished his studies in 1592, he found that his father had plans for him – in the shape of a wealthy Savoy heiress whom he wanted his son to marry. As we shall see, Francis eventually did have a profound relationship with a woman, but it wasn't this carefully selected Savoyarde.

Francis knew his destiny lay in a direction different to marriage: in 1593 he joined the cathedral chapter at Geneva in Switzerland and set about the arduous task of trying to convert the Protestant population of Chablais, a region on the southern side of Lake Geneva. This was dangerous work. The divisions and hatreds caused by the Protestant Reformation were still keenly felt in the region.

Francis travelled on foot, braving ice, snow, wolves and attacks by Protestant peasants. He preached in crumbling, nearly empty churches and distributed his own pamphlets. His greatest weapon was his personal conduct: people were struck by the way he spoke and lived his life, as well as his kindness, gentleness and modesty, and as a result, many returned to the Catholic faith.

In the years that followed, Francis continued to impress his superiors, and in 1602 the pope appointed him bishop of Geneva. Two years later, while he was preaching in Dijon in eastern France, he met a young widow named Jeanne de Chantal, who had had a vision that Francis would become her spiritual director.

This duly occurred, and the two of them became bound by a deep friendship (Francis said, 'In Madame Chantal I have found the perfect woman, whom Solomon had difficulty in finding in Jerusalem.'). Together they went on to establish, in 1610, the Visitation Order, designed for women who were drawn to the spiritual life but were unwilling to bear the harsh regimes of traditional religious orders.

For the remaining 12 years of his life, Francis continued to impress everyone with his dedication to God and his fellow human beings. He died at the age of 56 on 28 December 1622, while visiting Lyons. He was officially proclaimed a saint 33 years later.

A way of meditating

Francis's thoughts on meditation are found in his *Introduction to the Devout Life*, a book based on a spiritual manual he wrote for one of his relatives. It still remains in print. As mentioned before, Francis was writing from the perspective of the Christian tradition and refers to prayer and God in a way that might put off non-believers. Even so, I think what he says can be helpful to anyone interested in the practice of meditation.

In what follows, I have kept Francis's references to 'God' and other specifically Christian terms, but have occasionally tried to show how these can be adapted for non-Christians. The principles behind the meditation are what is important.

Francis begins his guide to meditation with a few prefatory remarks: 'Devote yourself to an hour's meditation every day before a meal. If you can manage it, meditate early in the morning, when the mind is not so busy and still fresh from a night's sleep. Don't spend more than an hour.' And if, he says, you cannot meditate in the morning because of the pressure of business, try to do it in the afternoon, but not 'straight after eating, or you'll feel sleepy'.

The meditation starts when Francis suggests the meditator should be aware of the presence of God (which for non-Christians could be a divine presence, or for non-believers, perhaps a sense of an 'otherness' beyond them) and ask for His help. Being aware of the divine presence differs from prayer. In prayer we attempt a direct link to the divine with our thoughts and words. Being aware of the divine is more about being sensitive to the surrounding psychic atmosphere: a move from the realm of the verbal (prayer) to the non-verbal (meditation).

Is there a definitive way of becoming aware of the divine presence? Not really. It is more like taking an imaginative leap. Francis helps us with a striking simile: the divine presence is everywhere, just as 'birds flying in the sky always encounter air'. In other words we may not see it, but it is there, alive and sustaining, and we have to imagine it around us.

Being aware of the divine presence is one thing, but we need to have an emotional response to it – it cannot be just a concept, or a thought trapped inside the head. Francis keeps emphasizing that meditation lives or dies by our ability to *feel* and *experience* rather than to know and believe. Theologians and priests have no advantage over lay people, but for everyone it is a challenge. It is much easier to say, 'I believe in God' or 'I believe in Krishna' and repeat words of doctrine, than to feel their presence.

It takes faith to make the imaginative leap. 'What people do not see,' Francis says, 'they easily forget.' If blind men stood before a prince they would not see him and give him due respect. We, in turn, 'do not see God; and although our faith tells us He is present, because we do not see Him, we are too apt to forget Him and act as though He was far away'. So, before we meditate, we must 'rouse our souls to think of God's presence'. *Rouse our souls* – we have to make an effort to move from formulae of words to a deeply felt experience.

Another way of coming to feel the presence of God, Francis says, is by realizing that He is not only in the place where we happen to be, but also *inside us*, in our hearts and minds. So we carry the divine presence with us wherever we go.

Francis also says we can be aware of His presence simply by using our ordinary imagination and picturing God in the person of Jesus standing or sitting beside us, 'just as we might think of our friends, and fancy that we see or hear them at our side'. Whether on a train journey, or standing at the bus stop, or sitting at a work desk, we can picture our spiritual guide by our side, ready to give us help whenever we need it.

The 'interior picture'

Imagination plays a crucial role in Francis's meditation, and he encourages us to use it in a way reminiscent of what Carl Jung called the 'active imagination'. It means shutting your eyes and conjuring up a particular scene so vividly that you seem to enter and actively participate in it. It is a sort of self-guided daydream. Francis refers to it as the 'interior picture'. He says: 'If you want to meditate on Jesus on the cross, be an actual witness on Mount Calvary in your imagination, as though you could see and hear everything that happened during his passion.'

This technique could be applied to any scene. We could create an 'interior picture' of Gautama reaching enlightenment, for example, imagining him sitting under a tree, hearing the sounds of the forest and smelling the vegetation, and watching the seated, still figure, with a smile creeping across his face. Or, on a more secular note, we could make an 'interior picture' of, say, climbing up a mountain and seeing the landscape below becoming increasingly miniature, feeling the freshness of the air and a sense of liberation as we clamber over rocks.

In all cases the trick is to relax and start with one or two details. It is tempting to think that you have to imagine the whole scene at once, but this usually results in the mind going blank. But if you concentrate on one detail, then you have a starting point.

For example, you might imagine the eyes of Gautama – closed, or half-opened, or flickering – and then you might imagine the rest of his face seen from a distance not too far and not too near. You keep adding details and after a while the mind begins to take over and you find yourself picturing other things you would never have thought of. Eventually, the scene becomes more and more real, as if you are actually in it yourself. Experimentation is important, and patience too. If you're not used to this type of imaginative projection it can be slow at first.

Visual meditation does not work, Francis says, with abstract qualities, such as God's 'greatness', or 'goodness'. It is at its most effective when we concentrate on human scenarios – for example, Jesus turning water into wine at the wedding at

Cana, or the Buddha preaching his lotus sermon. The strong focus we bring to the visualization stops our thoughts from wandering, 'like shutting a bird inside a cage, or fastening a hawk by a leash'.

For Francis, conjuring up a human scene is the starting point for meditation, but there is more to it. He is keen to point out that emotionally involved visual meditation differs radically from the sort of stream of imagination we might get from reading a book: 'Meditation is different from study and common everyday thinking. These do not have the love of God or spiritual growth for their object, but some other end, such as acquiring learning or the power of argument,' he says. Meditators, on the other hand, will keep a tight focus on the interior picture of the meditation, and will reflect on it and 'feed on it, like a bee, which hovers over a flower for as long as it can extract honey from it'.

Actions speak louder than thoughts

Francis stresses that meditation is a holistic activity; that is to say, it impacts on the whole of our lives – our thoughts, emotions, desires, and so on. It is not just a leisure activity that we can take or leave, a hobby that makes us relaxed for an hour or so (though being relaxed is an important part of meditation).

For Francis, meditation is never self-indulgent or purely self-focused. It foments 'good desires' in us, such as loving our neighbours, or feeling more compassion for everything, or feeling shame for the bad things we have done in the past. Meditation heightens and accentuates the noble part of our characters, making us more aware of our capacity for doing good and inspiring us to act on that awareness.

Not only that, meditation should lead to positive actions. For example, meditating on the crucifixion and Jesus's cry to God to forgive his persecutors might inspire the idea of forgiving our own enemies. 'But that is not enough,' Francis says, 'unless you convert it into practical action and say to yourself, "If a neighbour or servant has been going around saying unpleasant things about me or treating me with disrespect, I will not get angry. Instead, I shall behave in such a way as to please and make my peace with them."' The awareness that arises from meditation is useless unless we act on it.

'A bouquet of devotion'

The last part of Francis's meditation sequence consists of thanking God for the thoughts and emotions inspired in us through our meditation and offering them to him. We should also ask him for a blessing so that we can put the fruits of our meditation into practice. Again, for non-believers, the equivalent might simply be to acknowledge the thoughts and emotions we have received and to feel grateful for them and to resolve to act on them. It is a sort of formal recognition that we have engaged in meditation and are now returning to our everyday lives, fortified, it is hoped, by our experience.

Finally, Francis recommends we end our meditation with what he calls 'a little bouquet of devotion', which he illustrates as follows: 'When walking in a beautiful garden, many people like to pick a few flowers, which they keep in order to enjoy their scent for the rest of the day. So, when your mind explores some mystery in meditation, it is a good idea to pick out one or two points that have specially caught your attention… and to smell them spiritually for the rest of the day.'

In other words, we can base our day around a meditation. With practice, the ability to visualize becomes easier and leads to a deeper emotional response. The images that have led to this response are there for us to call upon for the rest of the day and longer.

In summary, Francis wants us to enter into a specific visualization with all our being; it's not a case of simply musing on an uplifting scene, but entering it in a three-dimensional way, as if we are *actually there*. That is the only way it will affect us profoundly. Meditation is not about escaping reality, but helping our ability to engage in and affect reality; not about thinking things, but about feeling things, in order to do things positively.

J. KRISHNAMURTI: HEALING OUR DIVISIONS

'Unless you fundamentally bring about a change
in your daily life, have right relationship with each
other, live correctly, not be ambitious and so on,
there is no possibility for the ending of conflict
between human beings.'

J. KRISHNAMURTI

One of the world's oldest professions, if not *the* oldest, must be soldiering. In 2005 excavations at an archaeological site called Hamoukar in northeast Syria showed that an intense battle had taken place there in about 3500BC. It is the earliest evidence we have for a large-scale conflict in ancient Mesopotamia. Today, more than 5,500 years later, nothing much has changed, with modern Mesopotamia – the Middle East – still an area of friction and fighting.

Fighting and aggression seem to be part of the human condition. It is hard to think of a time in our history when organized warfare has not happened. There are outbreaks of peace, here and there, but even among nations nominally allied or at peace there is verbal aggression and mistrust, diplomatic rows and instances of spying.

In the Book of Isaiah in the Bible, there is a vision of the end of the world when war will no longer occur: 'He [God] shall judge between the nations, and rebuke many people; they shall beat their swords into plowshares, and their spears into pruning hooks; nation shall not lift up sword against nation, neither shall they learn war any more.'

Turning weapons into farm implements and not learning the art of war seem a distant prospect. It may never happen, or not before the modern version of Isaiah's swords and spears have created a nuclear winter. But that is no reason not to try to create conditions in our own lives that might help the bigger picture of national and international harmony, even if it is only adding a drop of water to an ocean.

The Indian thinker and speaker J. (Jiddu) Krishnamurti once suggested that war starts at home. That is, we are all responsible for it. How so? How could I, say, living in my little house in the middle of the countryside, being a good citizen, helping old ladies across the road, be responsible for the war in Bosnia or Afghanistan or wherever?

Surely he doesn't mean me?

Yes, he does. Krishnamurti said that the conflicts we see reported on television or in newspapers are simply reflections, on a large scale, of conflicts that happen inside every one of us. By coming to terms with our own personal conflict, our own inner violence and aggression, we are helping to eradicate warfare on the world stage.

I should say at this point that writing about J. Krishnamurti and what he said is very difficult to do because he always insisted that his words should not be interpreted by anyone. He wanted them to be read plain and simple, without commentators 'explaining' them in a seemingly authoritative way. On the other hand, he was keen for people to think about and question his words as much as possible. He hated the idea of being someone who laid down the law. He wanted to provoke people into thinking for themselves, and question the deepest assumptions they had grown up with. So, what follows tries not to commentate or explain Krishnamurti's words, but to report them as best as possible.

Krishnamurti's suggestion that war will not go away until we, as individuals, acknowledge our own aggression made a huge impression on me. The corollary is that we can go on protest marches, withhold our taxes and demonstrate outside embassies until we are blue in the face but war will continue, as it has always done. Which is not to say that voicing opposition to war is wrong; simply that it is not enough. *We have to change ourselves first.*

Of course, violence and aggression are not confined to the battlefield. They can happen at home as well. We often find ourselves in conflict with those we live with and can demonstrate violence in various guises, from verbal attacks and passive aggressiveness to physical abuse. Krishnamurti spoke ceaselessly about the root problems of issues such as domestic strife. His views on conflict are relevant not only to international warfare but to squabbles, friction, vendettas or outbreaks of hostility between ourselves and people we know well.

From theosophist to religious speaker

Krishnamurti had a strange life, and a long one. He was born in southern India in 1895 – the year Rudolf Diesel developed his diesel engine – and died in 1986, when the Voyager 2 space probe was sending back information about the planet Uranus. His family was poor and his mother died when he was ten. He seems to have been a dreamy child, unacademic and fond of nature.

His life changed dramatically in 1909. He was walking on a beach when he was spotted by an Englishman named Charles Leadbeater, who was a leading light in the Theosophical Society (a group who explored esoteric spirituality and the occult). Leadbeater claimed to see an aura of light around Krishnamurti that was so pure it convinced him that the young boy was going to be a great spiritual teacher, even the 'Lord Maitreya', an enlightened being who, the theosophists believed, would be incarnated on Earth to guide the human race.

From this point onward, the theosophists, with the initial consent of Krishnamurti's father, took the boy and his brother Nitya into their care. Krishnamurti was taught the principles of theosophy and groomed to be the great world teacher his mentors expected him to be. He became particularly attached to Annie Besant, the president of the theosophists, who treated him like a son.

As the years went by, Krishnamurti continued to be schooled in his role as the Maitreya. In 1911 the theosophists founded a new organization, the Order of the Star in the East, to promote the idea that the arrival of Lord Maitreya was imminent. Krishnamurti, meanwhile, began to give talks on spiritual themes and lead discussions with sympathetic audiences.

But during the 1920s, he became increasingly sceptical about theosophy and his role in it. His change of thinking came to a head in 1929, when, at a huge public meeting at Ommen in Holland, he publicly dissolved the Order of the Star. He effectively resigned, leaving thousands of theosophists disillusioned. Annie Besant was heartbroken.

But Krishnamurti did not retire from public life. On the contrary, he continued as a thinker and speaker, but articulating his own thoughts, not those of the theosophists. From the start he made it clear that he was attached to no religion, saying that 'truth is a pathless land, and you cannot approach it by any path whatsoever, by any religion, by any sect.'

Over the following decades he travelled around the world, speaking in America, India, Britain and elsewhere, articulating his ideas and promoting discussions about life's problems. He was still doing public speaking, at the age of 90, shortly before he died in February 1986.

Krishnamurti is an unusual 'sage' in that he insisted he was *not* a sage, a guru or a teacher. He did not lay down a philosophy and expect a body of adherents to follow it. He was more like the ancient Greek philosopher Socrates, who questioned everyone and everything. He also concentrated on the facts of living, not on abstractions. He was not interested in theories but in what people actually experience in their lives. He wanted to investigate why we are lonely, sad, angry, happy, selfish, envious, ambitious, violent, appeasing, and so on. That was the focus of his attention.

In talk after talk, discussion after discussion, he would explore a topic or theme, sometimes in small gatherings, sometimes in front of huge audiences. A small, birdlike, white-haired figure in his old age, he would speak fluently for exactly an hour, without notes, taking care over every word, before inviting questions.

Some of the themes he talked and wrote about over the years were to do with the conditioning of the mind, conflict and fear, but whatever the topic, he often seemed to return to the same essential problem: the sense of individuality – the 'I', 'me' or 'ego' that every person has – which makes us feel separate from everything and everyone else.

A sense of separation

Most of us want to assert the sense of 'being me' – perhaps by talking about ourselves in company, buying things that reflect our sense of importance, or, less negatively, by writing a memoir. This is part of human nature. But by establishing our sense of self, we automatically separate ourselves from other people and the world around us. My 'me', which I have carefully built up, naturally creates a division or a distance between myself and my brother or next-door neighbour, or even between myself and the tree in my garden.

This sense of separation can make us feel lonely, alienated and insecure. We feel cut off from people and things, so we try to build bridges, make friends and have some sort of connection to nature. We might find temporary relief in alcohol or drugs because it reduces the sense of separation: with a few whiskeys in us, we suddenly feel that everyone is our friend and we can speak our minds without any inhibition. That is until the cold dawn of sobriety returns us to our little ego-shell of separation.

Most of us do not realize just how much we assert ourselves and build up our egos during the course of a day, a week or a year. Every time we hear of a friend's success and feel jealous it is our 'me' that is hurt; when we receive praise for a job well done it is our me that feels pleased; when we cannot overtake a slow-moving car it is our me that feels frustrated and angry. We live in a world of me without being aware of it most of the time.

And yet at some level we *are* aware of it. Because we feel cut off by making ourselves separate, we instinctively want to belong to something or someone or a group. I embrace my family, say, or my partner and my kids; I identify myself with my town or a football team, or a religion or a country. There is always some group – a club, religious sect, society, team, tribe, nation – that makes us feel part of a family and special, loved or wanted.

So, there arises a sort of equation:

The more we strive to assert the me,
the more we feel separate,
therefore the more we try to embrace
or identify with a group.

Divisions and conflict

This is where conflict comes in. What happens if I, feeling separate and insecure, identify myself with a particular group? Krishnamurti puts it like this: 'Where there is division as the Arab and the Jew, the Hindu and the Muslim, and so on, where there is division, there must be conflict. This is a natural law, which is what is actually taking place in the world. Why is there this division? Who has brought this about?'

This is a typical Krishnamurti utterance: stating the facts of *what is* (to use his phrase) – and it is hard to deny that *what is* consists of the divisions he describes – then ending not with a solution but with a question. He invites us to reflect, and not just accept a solution handed down from on high. Only by making the realization ourselves can we change ourselves; otherwise we might agree intellectually with an argument but not act on it.

Krishnamurti points out the obvious divisions that exist in the world: the divisions of race, such as Arab and Jew, and the divisions of religion, such as Hindu and Muslim. He could have added many more – divisions based on social class, for example, or politics, or financial income.

Some divisions we choose (for example a football team) and others we inherit.

For example, Jack is of Irish descent and was brought up as an American Catholic, while Jill is of Afro-Caribbean parentage and was raised as an American Baptist. When they meet, they find they have profound differences in the realm of their spirituality, governed by their respective conditioning. Where their conditioning overlaps, there is no issue; both, for example, cheer on the USA at the Olympics.

Krishnamurti asks us to consider the nature of being conditioned like Jack and Jill: 'Where there is conditioning, there must be conflict, because all conditioning is limited.' By conditioning being 'limited' I think he means that it puts us inside a particular box or cage (French, hippy, extrovert, Rastafarian, Mormon, Sri Lankan, Conservative, or whatever). He challenges us to remove the bars from our cage. If Jack loses his conditioning as a Catholic, and Jill loses her conditioning as a Baptist, there is one less barrier between them. If we all lost all our conditioning then how would conflicts between peoples, sects, religionists or football supporters be sustained?

The problem of conditioning

How do we lose our conditioning? The first step is to be aware of it. In some cases this is easy (if you are a committed Zoroastrian or a vegetarian, for example). But conditioning can be subtle: we are all probably more snobbish, class-conscious or class-envious than we are aware of. We have to get to know our conditioned prejudices and how we react when we encounter, say, someone with a skinhead haircut or speaking with a particular accent.

By observing our prejudices – which is often a painful process because we all think of ourselves as being more tolerant than we actually are – we get some sense of the range of our conditioning and what is dividing us from other people (class, race, religion, skin colour, fashion-sense, generation gap). This in turn builds up a picture of what our *me* is like, what our *me* has been conditioned by, and what its prejudices are.

With awareness of our conditioning comes a desire to change it, or react against it, or improve it: I realize I am a snob, so I try not to be one; I realize I'm prejudiced against people who like jazz music, so I try not to be. But, as Krishnamurti suggests, the trying *not* to be something is self-defeating, because the effort involved in trying serves in a strange way to strengthen our *me* ('I must like jazz fans, I must like hippies, I must not dismiss teenagers with punk hairstyles'): if the I, the me, is at the heart of the problem, it is also at the heart of the attempted solution – the trying to change.

So what do we do? Krishnamurti suggests that the 'me' is essentially 'the cause of conflict'. But if I ask how to be free of my 'me', I am asking the wrong question. What we must do is simply *observe* the entire process of our conflict – not attempt to grasp it – and it will tell us what we need to know.

As I understand it, this is the heart and the hardest part of the inward revolution we need to take that Krishnamurti hinted at so often. We observe our conflict, but instead of analysing it or taking an oath that we will try harder next time, we stop. We simply *continue observing*.

If we analyse it, it requires a *me* to do all that. Even a well-intentioned me is still a me – a thing that causes separation and conflict with others. If we do nothing but observe, be aware without commenting, analysing, judging or chattering (all of which bring the me to life), the me disappears and a new world beckons. We discover we are not isolated, lonely and alienated but part of a common humanity.

By steady awareness we change ourselves, and in doing so we remove conflict from our lives. We no longer feel hostile towards certain groups, sects or tribes because we no longer belong to a group, sect or tribe. Our personal transformation, Krishnamurti suggests, affects other people. If I meet someone who is free of conflict and full of love, compassion and intelligence I am naturally going to be affected by it.

Everyone can help to end conflict – the bullets, the bombs, the aggressive rhetoric, the torture, the spying, the whole paranoid edifice of 'national security' – simply by changing internally. We may or may not add our names to petitions or join protest marches, but what really matters starts in our own heads and hearts, as Krishnamurti says: 'When you as a human being radically transform psychologically, that is, be free of fear, have right relationship with each other… then you affect the whole consciousness of man.'

And of course, apart from helping the world to be a more peaceful place, an understanding of our conditioning is essential for good personal relationships with our family, friends and workmates. Charity, they say, begins at home, and so does the resolution of conflict.

FURTHER READING AND SOURCES

Each sage featured in this book could have a long bibliography devoted entirely to himself or herself, so I have just picked out a few titles that I found indispensable in writing this book and which I recommend for further reading.

Background surveys

For the lives and backgrounds of sages in the Christian mystical tradition, *Christian Mystics: Their Lives and Legacies throughout the Ages* by Ursula King (Hidden Spring, 2001) and *Love Burning in the Soul: The Story of the Christian Mystics, from St Paul to Thomas Merton* by James Harpur (Shambhala, 2005) are highly readable introductions.

Margery Kempe

The Book of Margery Kempe was written in Middle English, the language of Geoffrey Chaucer, and has been translated into modern English by various scholars, for example B.A. Windeatt (Penguin Books, 2000) and W. Butler-Bowdon (Jonathan Cape, 1936). It gives a fascinating insight into the life of a medieval woman, albeit an extremely unusual one.

For a glimpse of what Margery's original text looks like, visit http://www.lib.rochester.edu/camelot/teams/kemp1frm.htm. After a bit of tuning in, the text is relatively easy to understand, and the site has a helpful glossary. The quotes included in this book are my versions based on the sources mentioned.

Henry David Thoreau

Thoreau's account of his stay in the woods can be read in his classic *Walden*, re-issued by, for example, Oxford World Classics (edited and introduced by Stephen Allen Fender, 2008) or Dover Publications (1995). Thoreau can be a bit wordy, but his style is thoughtful and often memorably poetic. Chapter Five, 'Solitude', is particularly interesting for its insights into living alone. A good website for Thoreau and Walden is http://thoreau.eserver.org/wrkslnks.html#walden, which gives a selection of essays and articles on the book and the author, including background and historical and geographical information. It also gives the text of the book (http://thoreau.eserver.org/walden00.html).

Brother Lawrence

There is no better way to appreciate Brother Lawrence than to read his illuminating *Practice of the Presence of God*. The text is short and is widely available in an old translation by Donald Attwater (Burns, Oates and Washbourne Ltd., 1926), reprinted by various publishers (for example Oneworld, 1993). It can also be found online at http://www.ccel.org/ccel/lawrence/practice.toc.html. Another, more recent translation was made by E.M. Blaiklock (Hodder and Stoughton, 1981).

Plato

The allegory of the cave can be found in Book Seven of *The Republic* and it is well worth reading the (short) original account. There is a translation of it by the Victorian Oxford scholar Benjamin Jowett online at http://classics.mit.edu/Plato/republic.html. Jowett's language is slightly antiquated, so I also used H.D.P. Lee's translation of *The Republic* (Penguin Books, 1955) to formulate the words I quote. An excellent short claymation video of the allegory, written and directed by Michael Ramsey, can be found on YouTube at http://www.youtube.com/watch?v=69F7GhASOdM.

Mother Julian of Norwich

Mother Julian's *Revelations of Love* has been translated from Middle English into colloquial modern English by Clifton Wolters (Penguin Books, 1966) and, in an older version, by Grace Warrack (1901). The latter's translation, which I made use of, can be found online at http://www.ccel.org/ ccel/julian/revelations.html. It is also rewarding to get the flavour of Julian's original words, for example in *A Revelation of Love*, edited by Marion Glasscoe (University of Exeter Press, 1993). A website that offers background information and essays about Julian is http://www.luminarium.org/medlit/ julian.htm. An introduction to, and the text of, the *Ancrene Riwle* can be found at http://www.bsswebsite.me.uk/History/ AncreneRiwle/AncreneRiwle.htm. The piece from the *Riwle* that I quoted comes from Part Eight and has been modernized by me.

Carl Jung

Jung's thoughts on the shadow are scattered around his collected works, but the best introductory book to get an idea of him and his theories is his autobiographical *Memories, Dreams, and Reflections* (Fontana Press, 1967, with more recent reissues). This is a highly readable and engaging account of the major phases of Jung's life and the ideas he formulated. Another excellent book designed for the general reader is Jung's *Man and His Symbols* (Picador, 1978). Two good short introductions to his work are *An Introduction to Jung's Psychology* by Frieda Fordham (Penguin Books, 1966) and *Jung* by Anthony Storr (Fontana/Collins, 1973). A more weighty tome, which includes material on the shadow, is Jung's *The Archetypes and the Collective Unconscious* (Volume 9, Part 1, of the Collected Works, Routledge, 2nd edition, 1968), which can be bought in paperback (Routledge, 1980).

Jean-Pierre de Caussade

A good, readable translation of De Caussade's *Abandonment to Divine Providence* has been done by Kitty Muggeridge under the title *The Sacrament of the Present Moment* (Collins, Fount Paperbacks, 1981). There is also an older translation by E.J. Strickland (Herder Book Company, 1921). My own phrasing of quotations was based on the works of these two authors, along with reference to the French original. Strickland's translation can be found online at http://www.ccel.org/ccel/decaussade/abandonment.html. For those who know a little French, it is rewarding to read the original text at http://livres-mystiques.com/partieTEXTES/Caussade/Abandon.html. The poem by Horace quoted in the text is Book 1 Ode 11, and the version is by me.

Diogenes

The life of Diogenes occurs in Chapter Six of Diogenes Laertius's *Lives of Eminent Philosophers*. The translation by R.D. Hicks (Loeb, 1925), which I used, is available online at http://

en.wikisource.org/wiki/Lives_of_the_Eminent_Philosophers. The best general book on Diogenes is the excellent *Diogenes the Cynic* by Luis E. Navia (Humanity Books, 2005), which also includes Diogenes Laertius's account of Diogenes's life as an appendix. Navia gives the background to Diogenes and the Cynics and explores the main themes of Diogenes's philosophy in a scholarly yet readable account.

Hildegard of Bingen

There is a lot of material in print and online about Hildegard. But perhaps the best way into her is to listen to some of her music, of which there are many recordings. A good general biography, *Hildegard of Bingen: The Woman of Her Age*, has been written by Fiona Maddocks (Review, 2002), while Barbara Newman has edited a selection of essays (*Voice of the Living Light: Hildegard of Bingen and Her World*, University of California Press, 1998), which are scholarly and cover the different aspects of Hildegard's work. For Hildegard's own writings, *Scivias*, translated by Mother Columba Hart and Jane Bishop (Paulist Press, 1990), is indispensable. The quote from Hildegard's letter about Richardis is from Letter 64, Vol I, p.143 *The Letters of Hildegard of Bingen* (two vols) edited and translated by Joseph L. Baird and Radd K. Ehrman (Oxford University Press, 1998). The translation of *O nobilissima viriditas* is by me, and the song itself can be heard on YouTube.

Boethius

The *Consolation of Philosophy* has been translated by many people over the centuries. In recent times, Peter Walsh's version (Oxford Paperbacks, 2008) is excellent, as is that of V.E. Watts (Penguin Books, 1969). James Harpur's *Fortune's Prisoner* (Anvil Press, 2007) concentrates on the poems that complement the prose in the *Consolation* and also includes a useful introduction to the man and the book. The text of the *Consolation* can be found online in a translation by H.R. James (1897) at http://www.gutenberg. org/files/14328/14328h/14328-h.htm.

Jalaluddin Rumi

Rumi's poetry has been widely translated or been made into 'versions' (renderings based on existing translations). R.A. Nicholson translated the entire *Mathnawi* (E.J.W. Gibb Memorial Trust, 1926, with modern reprints) into what is considered to be accurate but slightly awkward English. E.H. Whinfield has published *Teachings of Rumi* (The Octagon Press, 1973), which comprises selections from the *Mathnawi*. In my chapter on Rumi I have done my own versions based on the words of Nicholson and Whinfield. For the Sufi background to Rumi, *The Sufis* by Idries Shah (The Octagon Press, 1964) is still a good introduction.

William Blake

Peter Ackroyd covers the ground of Blake's life in his *Blake* (Vintage, 2007), and the Blake scholar Kathleen Raine gives an excellent introduction to Blake's art in her *William Blake* (Thames & Hudson, 1970). David Bindman has produced a fine volume of Blake's original illuminated poems, which shows how Blake worked as a writer and artist simultaneously, integrating both of his gifts onto the page (*William Blake: The Complete Illuminated Books*, Thames & Hudson, 2000). Blake's poems can be found in the Penguin Classics edition (2004). A selection of his short, lyric poems can be found online at http://www.everypoet.com/archive/poetry/william_ blake/william_blake_contents.htm.

Li Bai

The best introduction to Li Bai (Li Po) is probably *The Selected Poems of Li Po,* translated by David Hinton (Anvil Press Poetry, 1998). Hinton gives the background to Li Bai's life and places him in the context of contemporary Daoist and Buddhist thought. Another fine translator from an older generation is Arthur Waley, for example his *More Translations from the Chinese* (Alfred A. Knopf, 1919), which can be found online at http://www.gutenberg.org/files/16500/16500-h/16500-h. htm#LI_PO. Waley's selection includes a handful of poems by

Li Bai. A more recent writer, Vikram Seth, included a selection of Li Bai's poems in his *Three Chinese Poets* (Faber and Faber, 1992). My own versions of Li Bai's poems are primarily based on translations by Hinton and Waley.

Marcus Aurelius

The *Meditations* is a book full of wisdom and repays close reading. It is rare to get an insight into the inner thoughts of anyone in the ancient world, let alone a Roman emperor. I used the translation of George Long (1862), which has been reissued (for example by Avon Books, 1993) and can be found online at http://classics.mit.edu/Antoninus/meditations.html, and I supplemented this with two more recent translations, one by Robin Hard (Wordsworth Classics, 1997), and Martin Hammond (Penguin Books, 2006). The latter two books include good introductions to Aurelius and the background to his thought.

St Francis de Sales

St Francis de Sales's *Introduction to the Devout Life* has been translated by John K. Ryan (Image Books, 1972, but available in more recent editions). Another, older, translation (Rivingtons, London, Oxford and Cambridge, 1876) can also be found at http://www.ccel.org/ccel/desales/devout_life. The section on meditation occurs in Part 2, Chapter 2, of the book. For French speakers, there is an edition of the book, *Introduction à la Vie Dévote*, published by Editions du Seuil (1995). I used the online text in conjunction with Ryan's translation.

J. Krishnamurti

There are numerous books of the teachings of Krishnamurti, but probably the two best ones to start with are *The Penguin Krishnamurti Reader* edited by Mary Lutyens (Penguin Books, 1970) and *The Second Penguin Krishnamurti Reader*, also edited by Lutyens (Penguin Books, 1973). These give a good idea of the range of topics Krishnamurti explored and discussed. Lutyens also wrote a number of biographical books about Krishnamurti, for example *The Life and Death of Krishnamurti* (John Murray, 1990). A very good website giving standard information about Krishnamurti is http://www.jkrishnamurti.org/index.php. For the specific topic of conflict, I referred most to Krishnamurti's third public talk in Saanen in the Netherlands (1971) and his second talk in New Delhi (1982). These two talks can be found online respectively at http://www.jkrishnamurti.org/krishnamurti-teachings/view-text.php?tid=1004&chid=706 and http://www.jkrishnamurti.org/krishnamurti-teachings/view-text.php?tid=37&chid=355&w=conflict